WE'D LIKE YOUR HELP!

We're working to make the best-possible text materials available to students. We want to know how well this textbook is working for you. Please keep this form until your course is completed. Then answer these quick questions, and mail it back. Thanks for your help!

1. **What is the title and edition number of the textbook you are using?** _____

2. **What is your purpose for taking this course? Are you:**

   _____ preparing for a new career?

   _____ preparing for the broker's exam or to become a broker?

   _____ preparing for career advancement?

   _____ completing part of a general business degree/program?

   _____ seeking information for personal use?

3. **Please rate this textbook on the following:**

Features	Excellent	Good	Fair	Poor
Easy to read	_____	_____	_____	_____
Accurate	_____	_____	_____	_____
Illustrations/Figures	_____	_____	_____	_____
Current	_____	_____	_____	_____
Other_____	_____	_____	_____	_____

4. **What chapters or topics did you find the hardest to understand?** _____
   _____
   _____

5. **How else can we make this book a better learning tool?** _____
   _____
   _____

Name/Address_____

School_____

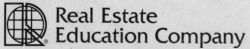

**Real Estate
Education Company**

a division of Dearborn Financial Publishing, Inc.

520 North Dearborn St., Chicago, IL 60610-4354

Phone 312-836-4400 FAX 312-836-1021

NOTE: This page, when folded over and taped, becomes an envelope, which has been approved by the United States Postal Service. It is provided for your convenience.

IMPORTANT—PLEASE FOLD OVER—PLEASE TAPE BEFORE MAILING

Return Address:

_____

_____

_____

No Postage
Necessary
if Mailed
in the
United States

BUSINESS REPLY MAIL

FIRST CLASS MAIL   PERMIT NO. 88176   CHICAGO, IL

POSTAGE WILL BE PAID BY ADDRESSEE:

Real Estate Education Company

a division of Dearborn Financial Publishing, Inc.

Attn: Marketing Department
520 North Dearborn Street
Chicago, Illinois 60610-9857

IMPORTANT—PLEASE FOLD OVER—PLEASE TAPE BEFORE MAILING

NOTE: This page, when folded over and taped, becomes an envelope, which has been approved by the United States Postal Service. It is provided for your convenience.

REAL ESTATE
MATH

Fourth Edition

Explanations
Problems
Solutions

REAL ESTATE
MATH

Fourth Edition

Explanations
Problems
Solutions

George Gaines, Jr. & David S. Coleman

REAL ESTATE EDUCATION COMPANY
a division of Dearborn Financial Publishing, Inc.

While a great deal of care has been taken to provide accurate and current information, the ideas, suggestions, general principles, and conclusions presented in this text are subject to local, state, and federal laws and regulations, court cases, and any revisions of same. The reader is thus urged to consult legal counsel regarding any points of law—this publication should not be used as a substitute for competent legal advice.

Published by Real Estate Education Company,
a division of Dearborn Financial Publishing, Inc.

Library of Congress Cataloging-in-Publication Data

Gaines, George.
    Real estate math : explanations, problems, solutions / George Gaines, Jr., David S. Coleman. — 4th ed.
        p.   cm.
    Third ed. published under title: Basic real estate math.
    Includes index.
    ISBN 0-7931-0134-4
    1. Business mathematics—Real estate business. I. Coleman, David S. II. Gaines, George. Basic real estate math. III. Title.
HF5716.R4G35   1990
333.33′01′513—dc20   90-36070
                                                          CIP

TABLE OF CONTENTS

YOU and This Book

Since virtually every real estate transaction involves numbers, it follows that everyone in the real estate business should know how to work with numbers. This book will help both prospective and existing real estate practitioners to become more confident when using figures. It will assist in sharpening the use of simple mathematics (hereafter referred to as "math") in general and in the field of real estate in particular. The book is especially designed for those who are preparing to take one or more examinations leading to a real estate license.

SPECIFIC PURPOSE

The aim of this book, therefore, is to help *you* become more comfortable with math basics as they are used in the real estate business. Little or no prior knowledge of either the math or the real estate field is assumed.

GENERAL ORGANIZATION

This book has been carefully arranged to help you gain skill in solving problems involving numbers. First, you will find an *explanation* in nontechnical terms of a particular math area. Next, you will encounter one or more examples and practice *problems* directly illustrating the math point just explained. And finally, you will be provided with *solutions* to all problems so that you will know immediately how you did.

Every effort has been made to keep the explanations, problems, and solutions relevant, accurate and success-focused. The authors want the conscientious student to be able to acquire the necessary skills to feel at ease when confronted with real estate situations involving the use of math.

THE PARTS OF THIS BOOK

At the beginning (Table of Contents) and at the end (Index), you will find the means to locate quickly the key points covered in this book. To aid you in assessing your level of understanding *before* you launch into the study of the material, a Pre-Test is included. To help you determine how well you have grasped the material *after* you have studied it, Post-Tests are offered. In between are eight chapters that start with the fundamentals (essentially Chapters 1 and 2), progress through math applications in specific parts of real estate activities and culminate in the final chapter, which brings together much of what has preceded it.

OTHER IMPORTANT PARTS

At the end of six of the chapters, a number of Review Problems have been designed to test your understanding of the contents of those chapters. Definitions of Key Math Terms, Symbols and Measurements appear at appropriate places in this combination math textbook and workbook. Since this is a math book and not a real estate principles and practices text, explanations of real estate terms are minimal.

HOW TO USE THIS BOOK

Work your way systematically through this book. Each chapter is designed to build on what has preceded it. Just reading the material once over lightly constitutes neither studying nor learning. Take the time and make the effort; you will learn and remember what you studied.

Study the explanations and examples thoroughly before attempting the practice and review problems. Once you begin to work the practice and review problems and are completely satisfied with your skill level in a particular subject area, you may choose to disregard solving any remaining such problems and move on to the next subject. If for any given problem you cannot arrive at the correct solution as indicated in the Answer Key, refer back to the chapter where the applicable concept is explained and illustrated.

Throughout this book, you will discover opportunities to express certain elements differently than the authors have. For example, just as "one half" may be written ½, 1/2, 0.5 or .5 and have the same meaning, so may a formula be expressed in different ways without changing its meaning or a problem may be approached differently and yet result in the same answer.

It will be tempting to use a calculator for many of the problems. The authors urge you to make certain that, first of all, you are able to solve the problems without a calculator. However, you then could usefully check your work with one. Calculators are a great aid in the business and you should know how to use one.

REACTION QUESTIONNAIRE

The authors want to know how well this book has met *your* individual needs. A preaddressed, return sheet may be found at the back of the book. Your comments are earnestly solicited so that future editions may be improved to meet more fully the needs of those who follow you.

George Gaines, Jr.
David S. Coleman

August, 1990

Parents! Do not miss the opportunity to have your children read and work the Pre-Test and Chapters 1 and 2 (perhaps 3) to help them, and you, find out if they know the basics of arithmetic.

PRE-TEST

The following survey is intended to help you determine those areas needing the greatest amount of study. Allow yourself about 45 minutes to take this pre-test. Do not use a calculator. Do not turn to the answers in the back of this book until you have finished this pre-test. If you score 80 or higher, you may want to be selective in using the material in this book. If you score below 80, you probably should study all of the material carefully.

- - - - - -

	Your Answer	Possible Score	Your Score

1. Reduce to simplest form: $\dfrac{46}{78}$ = $\dfrac{23}{39}$ 2   _____

2. Complete the individual math operation indicated:

   a. $3\dfrac{1}{12} + 8 + 1\dfrac{1}{3}$ = $12\dfrac{5}{12}$ 2   _____

   b. $\dfrac{2}{4} - \dfrac{4}{9}$ = $\dfrac{18}{36} - \dfrac{16}{36} = \dfrac{2}{36}$ $\dfrac{1}{18}$ 2   _____

   c. $\dfrac{2}{3} \div \dfrac{1}{4}$ = $\dfrac{2}{3} \times \dfrac{4}{1} = \dfrac{8}{3} = 2\dfrac{2}{3}$ 2   _____

   d. $\dfrac{5}{6} \times \dfrac{12}{15}$ = $\dfrac{2}{3}$ 2   _____

3. Convert to an improper fraction: $4\dfrac{11}{16}$ = $\dfrac{35}{16}$ 2   _____

4. Convert to decimal form:

   a. $\dfrac{16}{20}$ = $.8$ 2   _____

   b. $\dfrac{5}{4}$ = 1.25 2   _____

5. Convert to percent form:

a. $\frac{1}{3}$ = _33 1/3 %_   2 _____

b. $\frac{3}{5}$ = _60 %_   2 _____

6. Convert to fractional form:

a. 150% = _3/2_   2 _____

b. 5% = _1/20_   2 _____

7. Convert to decimal form:

a. 12½% = _.125_   2 _____

b. 122% = _1.22_   2 _____

8. 125.4 + .65 + 1.66 + 22 = _149.71_   2 _____

9. 24.19 − 6.234 = _17.956_   2 _____

10. 428.78 × 2.03 = _870.42_ (rounded to nearest hundredth)   2 _____

11. 5 2/5 × 3.25 = _17.55_   2 _____

12. 374.2 ÷ 1.871 = _200_   2 _____

13. 3.12 ÷ 293.04 = _.0106_ (rounded to nearest ten thousandth)   2 _____

14. 17.01 ÷ 3½ = _4.9_ (rounded to nearest tenth)   2 _____

15. You borrowed $20,000 at 10% interest for 2½ years. When you paid the loan and interest at the end of the loan period, how much did you pay the lender? _25,000_   4 _____

16. A weekly magazine subscription costs $41.60 per year. The same magazine sells for $2 per issue at the newsstand. How much will you save on each magazine if you subscribe? _1.20_   2 _____

What is this saving expressed as a percent:

 per magazine? _60 %_   2 _____

 annually? _60 %_   2 _____

17. How many 3-cent stamps are there in a dozen? ___12___   2   *2*

18. Last year, you weighed 120 pounds. This year, you weigh 135 pounds. What is the percent of increase in your weight? _12½ %_ ✓   5   _____

19. A salesperson works for a broker on a 60/40 commission basis (60% to the broker, 40% to the salesperson). The salesperson *45,000* sells 50 acres of land at $900 per acre. The gross sales commission is 10% of the sale price. What will the broker's commission be from the sale? ___$2700___   ✓4   _____

20. The sales commission earned by the broker who sold a building lot at a selling price of $22,000 was $1,980. What was the sales commission rate? ___9%___   ✓4   _____

21. At the end of 1½ years, you repay the bank $16,800, which includes $1,800 interest. What was the interest rate? _8%_   ✓5   _____

15,000) 1.5 yrs) —

22. What will the annual premium be for an insurance policy in the amount of $25,000 if the cost is $.60 per $100? _$150_   ✓4   _____

23. A developer is subdividing a 12-acre tract into lots measuring 80′ x 110′. Each lot has a perimeter of 380 feet and will sell for $4,500. He has allowed 126,720 square feet for required streets, sidewalks and recreational facilities. What is the area of each lot in square feet? ___8800___   ✓2   _____

How many salable lots will be realized? ___45___   ✓4   _____

24. Ms. Garcia's monthly mortgage payment for principal and interest is $264.60. If her annual property taxes are $780 and her 3-year homeowner's insurance premium is $594, what will *65 / 49.50* her total monthly payment be, including taxes and insurance? ___$346.10___   ✓4   _____

25. A rectangular-shaped lot has a frontage of 90 feet and a total area of 3,150 square yards. What is the depth of the lot? _315′_   ✓4   _____

26. You bought a vacant lot for $3,000. Six months later, you sold it for $2,700. What is your loss expressed as a percent? _10%_   ✓5   _____

27. Old MacDonald wants you to sell his farm. He wants to realize a net amount of $126,000 and agrees to a 10% sales commission. What must the sale price be for Old MacDonald to receive $126,000? ___140,000___   ✓5   _____

100

126,000 ÷ 90%

TOTALS: _150_

xiii

© 1979 United Feature Syndicate, Inc.

Chapter 1

Review of Basics*

A woman in a small town in Oklahoma uses a folksy expression to indicate her displeasure with someone else: "He acts like he lives 10 miles out of town and don't take a newspaper!" Now she could say "lives a ways out of town" or "lives far out of town," but she inserts a number in her statement. Why? The use of a definite number lends a certain factual authority to an otherwise vague personal opinion.

NUMBERS AND DIGITS

Numbers are used each day by every one of us to communicate with one another. Suppose your spouse leaves a note asking you to fill the car with gas and pick up a dozen eggs and a half pound of cheese. Not a single number was actually used, but look at the numbers that are directly and indirectly involved. Do you have enough money? How far will you have to drive? How much time will it take? The answers to all of these questions, as well as the quantity and cost of eggs and cheese, involve numbers.

The point is simply that there is no need to be uneasy about the use of numbers. You already use numbers all the time. Numbers are merely symbols to express ideas. Just as "music" is a term to indicate a system for the orderly expression of notes, "math" is a term to indicate a system for the orderly expression of numbers. The result of a lack of "system" in either music or math is a headache!

The symbols 0, 1, 2, 3, 4, 5, 6, 7, 8 and 9 are *digits*. You can combine them and arrange them to form an unlimited number of ideas, just as you can combine and arrange the letters A, B, C, D, etc., to express countless ideas in the form of words. When you select letters of the alphabet, for example, an A, a D, an L and an N to form the word LAND, you have arranged the letters to express a thought. You do the same with digits.

Digits are used to form *numerals*. Can you think of any words with only one letter of the alphabet? Of course you can—*I* can think of *a* couple! Numerals are formed in exactly the same manner. A numeral may consist of only one digit, or it may be composed of a great many digits. It is important to remember that the digits 0, 1, 2, 3, 4, 5, 6, 7, 8 and 9 are all available for use. For example, 9 is a numeral if it expresses the idea desired, and 9,999,999 is also a numeral. (Hereafter, numeral and number will be used interchangeably.)

Proper order is important in the use of numbers. For example, although the very same digits are used in 1,009 and 9,001, the order (arrangement of digits) causes the latter number to express a far greater value and a very different thought than the former number.

---

*If you feel confident that you know the material covered in this chapter, skip the chapter, or any portion you fully understand, and move on to the next part or chapter.
Regarding the use of a calculator, please read the note at the bottom of page 8.

PLACE VALUES

To ensure understanding and uniformity, the location of digits in a numeral determines their *place value*. Place value means the relative value or weight given a digit because of its position in a number. A *decimal point* is the dot located immediately after the units place to show that place values to its right are less than 1. The word *decimal* means based on the number 10. If no decimal point is written, then a decimal point is always regarded as located to the right of a numeral immediately after the last digit (the units place). A digit's relationship to the decimal point—written or unwritten—determines that digit's place value. For example, the second digit to the left of a decimal point has a place value ten times greater than the place value of the first digit to the left of the decimal point. The third digit left of the decimal point has a relative value one hundred times the place value of the first digit. This concept is illustrated below:

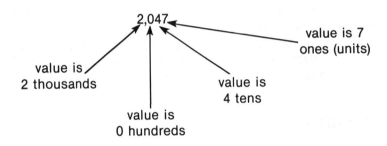

A value scale has been established for standardizing the place values of whole digits used in forming numbers. The farther left of the decimal point a digit is located, the greater its relative value:

Place Value Scale

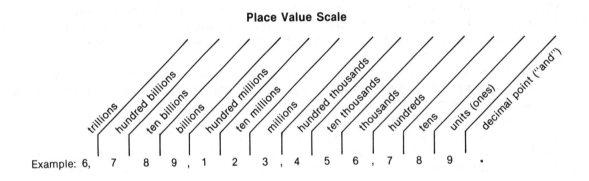

Notice the use of commas in the above whole number example. Moving from the decimal point to the left, a comma may be inserted between the third and fourth digits, another between the sixth and seventh digits, etc. It is much easier to read and use numbers having four or more digits when they are separated by commas than when they are not separated (6,789,123,456,789 versus 6789123456789).

Commas are not used to the right of the decimal point, regardless of the length of the decimal number (3,426.36412).

Now that you know the place value assigned to each digit in the numeral under the scale, write that complete numeral in words instead of digits:

_____

_____

Did you write: six trillion, seven hundred eighty-nine billion, one hundred twenty-three million, four hundred fifty-six thousand, seven hundred eighty-nine? If you did, you are correct.

Note that the word "and" is not used in writing whole numbers, even long numbers. For example, 934 is not expressed as nine hundred and thirty-four. To be correct, say and write nine hundred thirty-four. Then there is no doubt about the number. Do you follow this rule when writing checks?

The word "and" indicates the location of the decimal point and marks the exact location where a whole number ends and where a part of a whole number, called a decimal fraction, begins. A *whole number* may be defined as a digit from 0 to 9 or a combination of digits, such as 28 or 17,567. A *decimal fraction* may be defined as a part of a whole unit, such as .4 or .8642. A *mixed number* is a combination of a whole number and a decimal fraction or a common fraction, such as 6.25 or 6¼. A *common fraction* can express the same numerical value as a decimal fraction but in a different form. Common fractions will be explained in the next chapter.

To express an idea more precisely than is permitted by whole numbers, decimal fractions may be used. Decimal fractions extend the capabilities of the whole number system by indicating fractional parts of a whole unit. How would you like a monetary system restricted to whole units only—no fractional parts of a dollar allowed? A stamp would be a dollar, a cup of coffee would cost a dollar, etc. Fortunately, the United States monetary system is a decimal system, which permits the use of fractional parts of a dollar in exchange activities.

Decimal fractions expand the usefulness and accuracy of the place value in the same way that our money system operates. It breaks a whole unit down into an almost infinite number of parts:

Place Value Scale

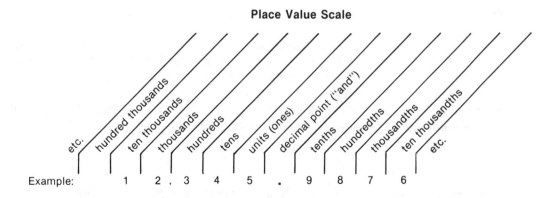

The correct way to write the number under the above scale is: twelve thousand, three hundred forty-five *and* nine thousand eight hundred seventy-six ten thousandths. Note: Commas are not used to the right of the decimal point, regardless of the length of the decimal number (3,426.36412).

Remember that all digits to the right of a decimal point make up a decimal fraction, and they represent a numerical value less than 1.

To test your understanding of place values, write each of the following numerals in words:

4,296 _____ 1-1

.0184 _____ 1-2

758,420 _____ 1-3

ROUNDING NUMBERS

How would you like to live in a world that insisted 72.96821 had to be written or spoken in complete terms? Thank goodness that our daily activities do not normally demand such precision. But you are called on to achieve various degrees of exactness in different situations. For example, in some situations, a less precise numerical value could be given, and thus the above number would be expressed as 73. In other cases, more precision may be required, but perhaps not to the extent of having to use all five decimal places, as in the above example. The *rounding place* digit is the one that indicates the degree of accuracy desired. For example, when rounding the above decimal number to hundredths, the digit 6 (in the hundredths position on the place value scale) is the rounding place digit. Once you decide on the degree of accuracy that is necessary, use the following rules as guidelines for *rounding* numbers:

Rule 1   The digit in the rounding place may stay as it is or change:

   a. If the digit in the rounding place has a 0, 1, 2, 3 or 4 to its immediate right, the rounding place digit is not changed and Rule 2 below applies. Ignore all other digits to the right of the rounding place digit.

   b. If the digit in the rounding place has a 5, 6, 7, 8 or 9 to its immediate right, the rounding place digit is increased by one and Rule 2 below applies.

Rule 2   It makes a difference whether whole numbers or decimal fractions are being rounded:

   a. When *rounding a whole number*, all digits to the right of the rounding place digit are replaced by zeros. For example, when rounding 973 to the nearest hundred, the digit 9 is in the hundreds position as established by the place value scale. Thus, the digit 9 is the rounding place digit. To the immediate right of the rounding place digit is a 7. As stated in Rule 1b above, the rounding place digit is increased by one, and both the 7 and the 3 are replaced with zeros. Thus, 9 becomes 10, two zeros replace the 7 and 3, and the result is 1,000 (973 rounded to the nearest hundred).

b. When *rounding a decimal fraction*, all digits to the right of the rounding place digit are dropped and are not replaced by any other digits. For example, when rounding .973 to the nearest hundredth, the digit 7 is in the hundredth position as established by the place value scale. Thus, the digit 7 is the rounding place digit. To the immediate right of the 7 is a 3. As required by Rule 1a above, the rounding place digit is not changed, the 3 is dropped and the result is .97 (.973 rounded to the nearest hundredth).

Rounding numbers is easier in practice than the above description would indicate. Although the rules may seem complicated, it may help to remember that rounding reduces the accuracy of a number value and replaces it with a more generalized value. "There were 973 people in attendance" is a more accurate count than "There were about 1,000 people in attendance" (rounding to the nearest hundred).

Appraisers in all fields frequently must round off their estimates to the nearest hundred dollars. For example, if an appraiser's computations produce the numeral $46,461, he or she would normally round that number to the nearest hundred dollars, or $46,500. To leave his/her appraisal at $46,461 would imply an accuracy not often possible.

Practice: Round 52,487 to the: nearest hundred _____

                    nearest thousand _____

First, note that you are rounding a whole number to the nearest hundred. Which is the rounding place digit? Counting from the right (units, tens, hundreds), you determine that the digit 4 is the rounding place digit. There is an 8 to its immediate right. Applying Rule 1b for rounding, you increase the 4 to a 5 and substitute zeros for all digits to the right of the rounding place as stated in Rule 2a. Thus, rounding 52,487 to the nearest hundred becomes 52,500.

Second, in rounding 52,487 to the nearest thousand, you find that the digit 2 is in the thousands position in the numeral. Thus, 2 becomes the rounding place digit when rounding to the nearest thousand. Since the number immediately to the right of the rounding place is 4, you apply Rule 1a and leave the rounding place digit unchanged. Then apply Rule 2a by substituting zeros for all whole numbers to the right of the rounding place digit 2. Thus, rounding 52,487 to the nearest thousand becomes 52,000.

Round 6.0448 to the nearest tenth: _____

The nearest tenth indicates that the rounding place will be the first digit position to the right of the decimal point. Decimal fraction rules apply. A look at the tenths position on the place value scale reveals that a zero is the rounding place digit in this example, with a 4 on the immediate right. Applying Rule 1a, the digit in the rounding place (0) must be left unchanged since Rule 2b states that the 4 (along with the digits to its right) should be dropped.

Note that all rules must be taken into account each time when rounding. Otherwise, a mistake is possible and inaccurate information may result.

Some will, no doubt, suggest that both the 0 and the 4 in the above example be dropped. To do so would ignore the degree of accuracy required. The question asked that 6.0448 be rounded to the nearest tenth. Therefore, 6.0 establishes accuracy between 5.95 and 6.04. If 6 is written, it indicates an accuracy somewhere between 5.5 and 6.4, which would be considerably less accurate than 6.0. In real estate, accuracy is not only a requirement but also a moral obligation when dealing with other people's property and money. In addition, answers on real estate examinations are frequently required to be exact.

The above discussion on rounding is based on classical and traditionally accepted practices. Several other approaches to rounding are employed by various industries and occupations. For example, statisticians use an odd/even digit method. Another school of rounding theory maintains that when rounding to the nearest cent, the rounding place is moved one digit right if the third digit from the decimal point is a 4. The criteria set by yourself or someone else often determine which method of rounding numbers is to be utilized. When dividing on a calculator, the answer will often need to be rounded before proceeding. Selection of the rounding place will determine the accuracy of the answer.

Definitions of the key math terms used in this chapter follow, along with 30 review problems to help you test your understanding of the material covered in this first chapter.

KEY MATH TERMS

Decimal: relating to the number 10; based on 10

Decimal Fraction: a digit or digits to the right of a decimal point (.6 or .738)

Decimal Point: the period or dot symbol located immediately after the units place to show that place values to its right are less than 1

Decimal System: a place-value method of using numbers based on 10. Each place to the left of the decimal point indicates that a number is raised to a higher power of 10, and each place to the right of a decimal point indicates division by 10.

Digit: any one of the symbols 0, 1, 2, 3, 4, 5, 6, 7, 8 or 9 used for writing numbers

Mixed Number: a numeral consisting of a whole number and a fraction (4½ or 4.5)

Numeral: a symbol or name for a number; a digit or a row of digits; a number

Place Value: the weight given a digit because of its position in a number

Rounding: expressing in approximate numbers rather than exact numbers

Rounding Place: in a number, the location of the digit that will determine the degree of accuracy desired

Whole Number: a digit from 0 to 9 or a combination of digits (7 or 36 or 43,560)

REVIEW PROBLEMS

Write each of the following numerals in words:

1. 4,345 _____

2. .005 _____

3. 6,253.17 _____

4. 2,450,050 _____

5. .0258 _____

Write each of the following in numerals, excluding common fractions:

6. Three thousand four hundred ninety-four and fifty-six hundredths

_____

7. Fourteen million one hundred sixty thousand two hundred twenty-one

_____

8. Ninety-eight million thirty-one

_____

9. Two thousand four hundred seventy and ten thousandths

_____

10. Six tenths

_____

Round each of the following numbers as indicated, using traditional math rules for rounding:

11. To the nearest thousandth   42.06948 _____

12. To the nearest tenth   .68743 _____

13. To the nearest hundredth   4.25389 _____

14. To the nearest cent $16.78392 _____

15. To the nearest hundred dollars $4,978.68420 _____

Write the name of the place on the value scale represented by the first digit of each numeral:

16. 4,697.32 _____

17. 926,843 _____

18. 10.09 _____

19. 4,222,613 _____

20. .796 _____

Write the name of the place on the value scale represented by the last digit on the right:

21. 21.34 _____

22. .9034 _____

23. 6.4 _____

24. .218967 _____

25. .34713 _____

Assume that the following statements are from your daily newspaper. Round each number in each sentence to a generally accepted degree of accuracy. Do *not* expect complete agreement by all as to the "answers."

26. The latest concept car will average about 68.7821 miles per gallon. _____

27. The population of the metropolitan area by 1995 will be 19,497,321. _____

28. The average cost per day of John Hill's homeowner's insurance policy is $.736982.

_____

29. In that state during the past year, the average homeowner's property taxes were $5.24547 per day.

_____

30. Mr. R. U. Shure appraised the three-bedroom house and lot at $63,458. _____

---

*As the introduction to this book indicates, the authors recommend that you demonstrate a firm grasp of the basics of each concept described by working the problems without the aid of a calculator. Once you are certain that you understand the math steps involved in a given problem area, then your numbers can be inserted into a calculator.

Chapter 2

Fractions, Decimals, Percent*

KEY MATH TERMS

Addition: the process used to find the sum of two or more numbers

   Sum: the result of adding numbers together

Subtraction: the process used to find the difference between two numbers

   Difference: the result of subtracting numbers; remainder

Multiplication: the process used to find the product of two or more numbers

   Product: the result of multiplying numbers together

Division: the process used to find the quotient of two numbers

   Dividend: a number to be divided

   Divisor: a number by which a dividend is divided

   Quotient: the result of dividing one number (the dividend) by another number (the divisor)

Fraction: part of a whole; may be expressed as a common fraction (¼) or as a decimal fraction (.25)

   Numerator: the part of a fraction which is above the line (signifies the number of parts of the whole unit being counted)

   Denominator: the part of a fraction which is below the line (signifies the total number of equal parts in the whole unit)

   Common Fraction: a number made up of a numerator and a denominator separated by a horizontal or diagonal line (1/4 or 5/5 or 8/3)

   Proper Fraction: a number in which the denominator is greater than ($>$) the numerator (3/8)

   Improper Fraction: a number in which the numerator is equal to or greater than the denominator (8/8 or 8/3)

---

*If you feel that you already know all of the material in this chapter, skip this chapter, or any portion of it, and move on to the next part or chapter.

Decimal: relating to (based on) the number 10; any number that has a written decimal point (.015 or 1.023)

Percent: per hundred; per hundred parts

Percentage: a part of a whole; an amount

Mixed Number: a whole number plus a fraction

KEY MATH SYMBOLS

=	equals	$<$	is less than
+	add	$>$	is greater than
−	subtract	°	degrees
×	multiply	′	minutes; feet
÷	divide	″	seconds; inches
%	percent	∟	right angle (90°)

MATH OPERATIONS

There are various ways to express each of the four basic math operations. For each one, all of the symbols and words shown mean to perform the same operation.

Addition:		+	and	plus
	Ex.:	4 + 3	4 and 3	4 plus 3
Subtraction:		−	minus	less	from
	Ex.:	4 − 3	4 minus 3	4 less 3	3 from 4
Multiplication:		×	·	times	( )
	Ex.:	4 × 3	4 · 3	4 times 3	4(3)
Division:		÷	⌐	into	$\frac{4}{3}$
	Ex.:	4 ÷ 3	3⌐4	3 into 4	

Since completing school, many adults have had little need to work closely with fractions, decimals and percents. However, real estate is a business that demands dealing with these math fundamentals on a daily basis. Real estate salespersons regularly confront property descriptions in which fractions are used (SE¼). They also regularly encounter decimals that appear with dimensions of properties (208.71 feet). Real estate people regularly see (or hope to see) sales commissions figured as a percent of the selling price (7%) as well as a percent of the total sales commission earned (40%).

The list of specific applications could go on and on, but suffice it to say that no real estate professional can adequately perform the necessary daily activities unless he or she has a working knowledge of these and other math basics. This chapter deals with fractions, decimals and percents in general and assumes little or no recent experience in these areas on the part of the student. The following chapters cover the use of these three numerical representations as they specifically apply to real estate.

FRACTIONS

When a whole unit, or number, is divided into equal parts, each of the parts is a fraction (and a percent) of the whole unit. For example, if a city block is divided into two equal parts, each of the parts is one-half (½) of a city block.

When dealing with fractions, the number below the line is called the *denominator*. The denominator always indicates the total number of equal parts in a whole unit. In the above example of the city block, the fraction ½ has as its lower number (denominator) the digit 2. This indicates a total number of 2 equal parts in the entire city block. If the fraction ¼ had been used, the denominator would have indicated that the city block was divided into 4 equal parts.

The number in a fraction that appears above the line dividing the numbers is called the *numerator*. The numerator indicates how many of the equal parts of the whole unit are being counted. For example, in the fraction 3/4, the numerator indicates 3 equal parts and the denominator shows a total of 4 equal parts, so you are talking about all but one equal part of something (all but ¼).

FRACTION:

$$\frac{2}{3} \quad \begin{array}{l}\text{Numerator} \\ \text{Denominator}\end{array}$$

The line separating the numerator from the denominator means division (the top number is divided by the bottom number).

A *proper fraction* is a part of a whole whose denominator is always greater than its numerator (½, ¼, 5/17, 21/22). An *improper fraction* is one whose numerator is equal to, or greater than, the denominator (4/4, 6/4, 12/3, 36/35). The term *common fraction* includes both proper fractions and improper fractions.

Changing Fractions

To change an improper fraction (when necessary) to a whole number or a mixed number, divide the numerator by the denominator.

Examples: $\frac{8}{4} = 2$ $\qquad\qquad \frac{8}{7} = 1\frac{1}{7}$

Practice: $\frac{9}{8} =$ $\qquad\qquad \frac{20}{5} =$ $\qquad\qquad$ 2-1
2-2

To change a mixed number to an improper fraction, multiply the whole number by the denominator, add the numerator and place that result over the denominator of the mixed number.

Sequence of steps: Example: 7½

First, multiply the whole number by the denominator: $7 \times 2 = 14$

Next, add the numerator: $14 + 1 = 15$

Then, place the result over the denominator of the $\dfrac{15}{2}$
mixed number:

Example: $12\dfrac{3}{4} = \dfrac{(12 \times 4) + 3}{4} = \dfrac{51}{4}$

Note: The parentheses in the above equation indicate that the enclosed math
procedure must be done first.

Practice: $2\dfrac{1}{7} =$ 2-3

$21\dfrac{2}{9} =$ 2-4

Reducing Fractions

To change a fraction that can be reduced without changing its value, divide both the numerator and the denominator by the same largest possible number, that is, the "greatest common factor."

Examples: $\dfrac{3}{12} = \dfrac{3 \div 3}{12 \div 3} = \dfrac{1}{4}$

$\dfrac{72}{84} = \dfrac{72 \div 4}{84 \div 4} = \dfrac{18}{21} = \dfrac{18 \div 3}{21 \div 3} = \dfrac{6}{7}$ or simply $\dfrac{72 \div 12}{84 \div 12} = \dfrac{6}{7}$

When the numerator and the denominator cannot again be divided evenly by a greatest common factor, the fraction is in its "simplest form."

Practice: $\dfrac{7}{21} =$ 2-5

$\dfrac{3}{36} =$ 2-6

Finding Common Denominators

Whenever denominators are not the same, fractions cannot be added or subtracted until a "common denominator" is found. The lowest number that can be divided evenly by all of the denominators is called the "lowest common denominator."

First, make certain that all fractions are in their simplest form. Then test for a common denominator by determining if all of the denominators will divide evenly into the largest denominator. For example, find the lowest common denominator for:

$$\frac{3}{4} \text{ and } \frac{1}{2} \text{ and } \frac{5}{8}$$

The largest denominator is 8, and the other two denominators (4 and 2) will divide evenly into 8. Thus, 8 becomes the lowest common denominator.

To restate the original fractions in terms of the new common denominator in the above example:

First, divide the new common denominator by each original denominator:

$$8 \div 4 = 2$$

$$8 \div 2 = 4$$

$$8 \div 8 = 1$$

Next, multiply each resulting answer (quotient) by the original numerator to obtain the correct new numerator:

2×3 (from 3/4) = 6 is the new numerator of the first fraction

4×1 (from 1/2) = 4 is the new numerator of the second fraction

1×5 (from 5/8) = 5 is the new numerator of the third fraction

Then, combine the new numerators with the common denominator (8):

$$\frac{3}{4} = \frac{6}{8}$$

$$\frac{1}{2} = \frac{4}{8}$$

$$\frac{5}{8} = \frac{5}{8}$$

Now the fractions are restated in terms of the lowest common denominator and are ready to be added or subtracted.

If this first test for finding the lowest common denominator does not work, test for a common denominator by multiplying the two smallest denominators involved. For example, find the lowest common denominator for:

$$\frac{1}{4} \text{ and } \frac{1}{6} \text{ and } \frac{1}{3}$$

The two smallest denominators are 4 and 3, and 4 × 3 = 12. Will all three denominators divide evenly into 12? Yes; thus 12 becomes the lowest common denominator.

If this second test does not work, try another pair of denominators, as shown in the following example:

$$\frac{1}{4} \text{ and } \frac{1}{6} \text{ and } \frac{1}{2}$$

Since the result of multiplying the two smallest denominators (4 × 2) is 8 and cannot be divided evenly by all denominators, the next largest pair (6 and 2) should be tried. This yields 12 and can be divided evenly by all three denominators.

When all of the above tests fail, multiply all of the denominators as shown in the following example:

$$\frac{3}{4} \text{ and } \frac{1}{7} \text{ and } \frac{2}{5}$$

In this problem, 4 × 5 does not work, 4 × 7 does not work, and 5 × 7 does not work in finding a common denominator. Thus, it becomes necessary to multiply all of the denominators (4 × 7 × 5 = 140). In this case, 140 is the lowest common denominator.

Note: If any of the fractions has not been reduced to simplest form, the result may not be the lowest common denominator, but it will yield a common denominator that can be reduced.

Practice: $\frac{3}{4}$ and $\frac{1}{8}$ The lowest common denominator is _____ .   2-7

$\dfrac{6}{8}$ and $\dfrac{4}{6}$ The lowest common denominator is _____ .   2-8

$\dfrac{3}{4}$ and $\dfrac{1}{7}$ and $\dfrac{3}{14}$ The lowest common denominator is _____ .   2-9

$\dfrac{1}{9}$ and $\dfrac{2}{7}$ and $\dfrac{1}{4}$ The lowest common denominator is _____ .   2-10

Adding and Subtracting Fractions

To add or subtract fractions, it is first necessary to determine the lowest common denominator as explained above. Then, add (or subtract) the new numerators and place the result over the common denominator. It may be necessary to reduce the resulting fraction to its simplest form.

Examples: Adding fractions—
(Find the common denominator and add the new numerators together. Place that sum over the new common denominator.)

$1/2 + 1/4 =$

$\dfrac{1}{2} = \dfrac{2}{4} ; \dfrac{1}{4} = \dfrac{1}{4}$

$\dfrac{2}{4} + \dfrac{1}{4} = \dfrac{3}{4}$ (called the sum)

Subtracting fractions—
(Find the common denominator and subtract the new numerators. Place the difference over the new common denominator.)

$1/3 - 1/5 =$

$\dfrac{1}{3} = \dfrac{5}{15} ; \dfrac{1}{5} = \dfrac{3}{15}$

$\dfrac{5}{15} - \dfrac{3}{15} = \dfrac{2}{15}$ (called the difference)

Practice: $\dfrac{2}{7} + \dfrac{12}{35} =$ 2-11

$\dfrac{14}{15} - \dfrac{1}{4} =$ 2-12

Multiplying Fractions

To multiply fractions, multiply the numerators, then multiply the denominators, place the product of the numerators over the product of the denominators, and reduce the fraction to its simplest form (if necessary).

Examples: $\dfrac{1}{4} \times \dfrac{5}{6} = \dfrac{1 \times 5}{4 \times 6} = \dfrac{5}{24}$ (called the product)

$$\dfrac{3}{5} \times \dfrac{4}{7} = \dfrac{3 \times 4}{5 \times 7} = \dfrac{12}{35}$$

Practice: $\dfrac{6}{11} \times \dfrac{3}{7} =$ 2-13

To multiply a whole number by a fraction, the whole number is treated as the numerator with a denominator of 1.

Example: $3 \times \dfrac{5}{12} = \dfrac{3}{1} \times \dfrac{5}{12} = \dfrac{3 \times 5}{1 \times 12} = \dfrac{15}{12} = 1\dfrac{3}{12} = 1\dfrac{1}{4}$

Some multiplication problems can be simplified by reducing numbers before multiplying. To reduce in preparation for multiplying, divide one numerator and one denominator by the same number, and then multiply as before. In the above example:

$$3 \times \dfrac{5}{12} = \dfrac{3}{1} \times \dfrac{5}{12} \text{ (the numerator 3 and the denominator 12 can both be divided by 3)}$$

$$\dfrac{\overset{1}{\cancel{3}}}{1} \times \dfrac{5}{\underset{4}{\cancel{12}}} = \dfrac{1 \times 5}{1 \times 4} = \dfrac{5}{4} = 1\dfrac{1}{4}$$

This crossing out of a number is called "canceling."

The following example shows the value of reducing to simplest form before multiplying:

$$\dfrac{7}{14} \times \dfrac{5}{12} \times \dfrac{3}{5} \times \dfrac{3}{8} =$$

If you multiply as is without first reducing, the problem progresses as follows:

$$\frac{7 \times 5 \times 3 \times 3}{14 \times 12 \times 5 \times 8} = \frac{315}{6,720} = \text{Try expressing this in its simplest form!}$$

But, if you reduce first and then multiply, the problem progresses as follows:

$$\overset{1}{\underset{2}{\frac{7}{\cancel{14}}}} \times \overset{1}{\underset{4}{\frac{\cancel{5}}{\cancel{12}}}} \times \overset{1}{\underset{1}{\frac{\cancel{3}}{\cancel{5}}}} \times \frac{3}{8} = \frac{3}{64}$$

Practice: $13 \times \dfrac{2}{11} =$ 2-14

$$\frac{1}{36} \times \frac{6}{12} \times 9 =$$ 2-15

   To multiply a mixed number by a fraction, convert the mixed number to an improper fraction (for method, see pages 11 and 12) and complete the problem as you would for the multiplication of fractions.

   Note: Canceling cannot be done until mixed numbers are converted into fractions.

Examples: $2\dfrac{5}{8} \times \dfrac{1}{2} = \dfrac{21}{8} \times \dfrac{1}{2} = \dfrac{21 \times 1}{8 \times 2} = \dfrac{21}{16}$ or $1\dfrac{5}{16}$

$$12\frac{1}{3} \times \frac{2}{3} = \frac{37}{3} \times \frac{2}{3} = \frac{74}{9} \text{ or } 8\frac{2}{9}$$

Practice: $4\dfrac{5}{7} \times \dfrac{4}{5} =$ 2-16

$$2\frac{1}{2} \times \frac{8}{15} \times 5 =$$ 2-17

Dividing Fractions

To divide fractions, invert (turn upside down) the fraction that you are dividing by (the divisor) and complete the problem as you would for the multiplication of fractions (see above).

Note: You cannot cancel out numbers until you are ready to multiply.

Example: $\frac{3}{4} \div \frac{1}{2} = \frac{3}{\underset{2}{\cancel{4}}} \times \frac{\overset{1}{\cancel{2}}}{1} = \frac{3 \times 1}{2 \times 1} = \frac{3}{2} = 1\frac{1}{2}$ (called the quotient)

Practice: $\frac{6}{7} \div \frac{2}{5} =$ 2-18

To divide a whole number by a fraction, invert the fraction that you are dividing by and complete the problem as you would for the multiplication of whole numbers by fractions (see above).

Example: $4 \div \frac{3}{5} = \frac{4}{1} \times \frac{5}{3} = \frac{20}{3}$ or $6\frac{2}{3}$

Practice: $17 \div \frac{1}{2} =$ 2-19

To divide a fraction by a whole number, place the whole number over the denominator 1 and complete the problem as above.

Example: $\frac{3}{5} \div 4 = \frac{3}{5} \div \frac{4}{1} = \frac{3}{5} \times \frac{1}{4} = \frac{3}{20}$

Practice: $\frac{1}{2} \div 11 =$ 2-20

To divide a mixed number by a fraction, convert the mixed number to an improper fraction (see above) and complete the problem as you would for the multiplication of fractions (see above).

Examples: $9\frac{1}{3} \div \frac{4}{5} = \frac{\overset{7}{\cancel{28}}}{3} \times \frac{5}{\underset{1}{\cancel{4}}} = \frac{35}{3}$ or $11\frac{2}{3}$

$7\frac{1}{2} \div 4 = \frac{15}{2} \div \frac{4}{1} = \frac{15}{2} \times \frac{1}{4} = \frac{15}{8} = 1\frac{7}{8}$

Practice: $10\frac{1}{5} \div \frac{2}{5} =$ 2-21

DECIMALS

In this section, the focus is on numbers in which the decimal point is involved.

Adding or Subtracting Decimals

To add or subtract decimals, vertically line up the decimal points under each other and add or subtract as you would with whole numbers.

Examples: Adding decimals — 1.2 + .05 =
$$
\begin{array}{r}
1.20 \\
+ \ .05 \\
\hline
1.25
\end{array}
$$

Subtracting decimals — 1.2 − .05 =
$$
\begin{array}{r}
1.20 \\
- \ .05 \\
\hline
1.15
\end{array}
$$

Practice: 23.16 + .067 =   2-22

11.26 − 1.3 =   2-23

Multiplying Decimals

To multiply decimals, multiply as you would whole numbers, add the total number of decimal places in all numbers being multiplied, and mark off the product from right to left accordingly. Zero(s) may have to be added to the left if there are not enough digits for the number of decimal places.

Examples:
$$
\begin{array}{r}
2.67 \text{ (2 places)} \\
\times \ \ \ 2 \text{ (0 places)} \\
\hline
5.34 \text{ (2 places)}
\end{array}
\qquad
\begin{array}{r}
.124 \text{ (3 places)} \\
\times \ \ \ .03 \text{ (2 places)} \\
\hline
.00372 \text{ (5 places)}
\end{array}
$$

Practice: 27.2 × 1.11 =   2-24

0.25 × .04 =   2-25

Dividing Decimals

To divide a decimal number by a whole number, place the decimal point in the answer space directly above the decimal point of the decimal number being divided (the dividend) and complete as you would regular division.

Example: 9.03 ÷ 3 = $\overset{\displaystyle 3.01}{3\,\overline{)\,9.03}}$

Practice: 18.15 ÷ 5 =   2-26

To divide a whole number by a decimal, first change the dividing number (divisor) into a whole number by moving the decimal point to the right of the last digit. Write the decimal point after the whole number being divided (the dividend). Then move that decimal point to the right the same number of places as you did with the dividing number (the decimal number you started with). Zero(s) will have to be added to the dividend. Next, place the decimal point in the answer space directly above the new location of the decimal point in the dividend. Complete the problem as you would regular division.

Example: 246 ÷ .2 = .2 $\overline{)\,246}$

          = .2 $\overline{)\,246.0}$ *or*   .2 $\overline{)\,246.0}$

          = 1,230

Practice: 3 ÷ .12 =   2-27

To divide a decimal by a decimal, first change the dividing number (the divisor) into a whole number by moving the decimal point to the right. Then relocate the decimal point in the number being divided (the dividend) the same number of places as you did with the divisor. Zero(s) may or may not need to be added. Place the decimal point in the answer space directly above the new location of the decimal point in the dividend, and complete as you would for regular division.

Examples: .246 ÷ .2 = .2 $\overline{)\,.246}$ = $\overset{\displaystyle 1.23}{.2\,\overline{)\,.2\,4\,6}}$ = 1.23

          .003 ÷ .3 = .3 $\overline{)\,.003}$ = $\overset{\displaystyle .01}{.3\,\overline{)\,.0\,0\,3}}$ = .01

Practice: .3 ÷ .12 =   2-28

Changing a Fraction to a Decimal

The line that is located between the two numbers of a fraction means divided by. Thus, ½ means 1 divided by 2. The rule for converting a fraction to a decimal is divide the numerator (top number) by the denominator (bottom number). Or if you wish, you can express the rule as divide the denominator into the numerator.

Example: $\frac{1}{5} = 1 \div 5 = 5\overline{\smash{)}1.0} = .2$

Practice: $\frac{3}{8} = \qquad = \overline{} =$ 2-29

Changing a Decimal to a Fraction

Knowledge of place value is necessary to convert a decimal into a fraction. With the decimal point removed, the number in question becomes the numerator and the place value of the last digit to the right becomes the denominator. The resulting fraction may or may not be in its simplest form. If it is not, it should be reduced.

Examples: $.25 = \frac{25}{100} = \frac{1}{4}$

$.123 = \frac{123}{1,000}$

Practice: $1.23 =$ 2-30

$.6 \quad =$ 2-31

PERCENT

Percent means by the hundred or per hundred parts. Thus, when you say 27 percent, you are actually saying 27 parts out of a possible 100 parts. Any percent figure less than 100 percent means a part, or fraction, of the whole. Any percent figure greater than 100 percent means more than a whole unit. For example, 125 percent means one whole (100 parts) plus 25 parts of a second whole. The symbol for percent is %. Any whole (total amount) can be expressed as 100%.

Changing a Percent to a Fraction or a Decimal

In the actual working of a problem involving percent(s), the percent figure(s) must be changed either to a fraction or a decimal.

To change a percent to a fraction, remember that a percent becomes a fraction when placed over its denominator of 100 (the whole to which it is related).

If the percent is a whole number, drop the percent sign, place the number as the numerator over 100, and reduce the resulting fraction, whenever possible.

Examples: $12\% = \frac{12}{100} = \frac{3}{25}$

$150\% = \frac{150}{100} = 1\frac{1}{2}$

Practice: $11\% =$ 2-32

$8\% =$ 2-33

If the percent is a mixed number:

    First, convert the mixed number to a decimal number:

    Next, place the decimal number over the denominator 100:

    Next, convert the decimal number in the numerator to a whole number by moving the decimal point to the right and adding a zero(s) to the denominator for each place the decimal point in the numerator was moved right:

Example: $7\frac{1}{2}\%$

$7\frac{1}{2}\% = 7.5\%$

$7.5\% = \frac{7.5}{100}$

$\frac{7.5}{100} = \frac{75}{1,000}$

Finally, reduce the fraction to its
simplest form:

$$\frac{75}{1,000} = \frac{3}{40}$$

Example: $8\frac{3}{4}\% = 8.75\% = \frac{8.75}{100} = \frac{875 \div 125}{10,000 \div 125} = \frac{7}{80}$

Practice: $10\frac{1}{2}\% =$ 2-34

To change a percent to a decimal, again remember that the percent sign is dropped and the number becomes a fraction when placed over its denominator of 100. Instead of reducing the fraction, divide the numerator by 100, which will result in a decimal number. Once the above procedure is understood, it is easier to drop the percent sign and just move the decimal point two places to the left because to divide by 100 means to move the decimal point two places to the left. If necessary, add a zero(s) to create the correct number of places the decimal point must move left.

Examples: $40\% = \frac{40}{100} = .40$ (long method)

$40\% = 40. = .40$ (shortcut)

$150\% = 1.50. = 1.50$

$7\% = 07. = .07$

$7\frac{1}{2}\% = 7.5\% = 07.5 = .075$

Practice: $24\% =$ 2-35

$1.1\% =$ 2-36

Changing a Fraction or a Decimal to a Percent

To change a fraction to a percent, first divide the numerator by the denominator. The result is a decimal. Move the decimal point two places to the right and add the percent sign.

Examples: $\frac{1}{4} = .25 = 25\%$

$2\frac{3}{4} = 2.75 = 275\%$

Practice: $\frac{1}{8} =$ 2-37

To change a decimal to a percent, move the decimal point two places to the right and add the percent sign.

Examples: 3.5   = 3.50 = 350%

             .007 = .007 = .7%

Practice: .23   =   2-38

As a final example of the previous number conversions, examine the following table carefully.

Percent	Decimal	Fraction Unreduced	Reduced
100%	1.00	$\frac{100}{100}$	$\frac{1}{1}$
70%	.70	$\frac{70}{100}$	$\frac{7}{10}$
3%	.03	$\frac{3}{100}$	$\frac{3}{100}$
$\frac{1}{4}$%	.0025	$\frac{25}{10,000}$	$\frac{1}{400}$

Practice by completing the following table.

Percent	Decimal	Fraction Unreduced	Reduced	
15%	.15	$\frac{15}{100}$	$\frac{3}{50}$	2-39
1.2%	.012	$\frac{12}{1000}$	$\frac{3}{250}$	2-40
6.25%	.0625	$\frac{625}{10,000}$	$\frac{1}{16}$	2-41
5%	.05	$\frac{5}{100}$	$\frac{1}{20}$	2-42

Percent in Problems

Now that the working relationships between fractions, decimals and percents have been explained and practiced, it is appropriate to turn to the use of percent as it is found in word problems.

Suppose something costs you $80 and you sell it for $100. What is your dollar profit? $ _____ What is your percent of profit? _____ %.

The answer to the first question is easy: $100 − $80 = $20 profit.

The answer to the second question is often given as 20%, which is wrong! "Profit" is how much you make over and above your cost. It may be expressed as an amount or as a percent of your cost.

The question about percent of profit is asking what part the profit ($20) is of your cost ($80). This relationship can be shown as the fraction $20/$80, which can be converted to a percent:

$$\frac{\$20}{\$80} = .25 = 25\% \text{ profit} \qquad \boxed{\frac{\text{made}}{\text{paid}} = \text{percent profit}}$$

To check the answer:

```
cost          =                 $ 80
profit        = 25% × $80 =       20
selling price =                 $100
```

If you had answered 20% instead of 25%, checking your answer would have revealed:

```
cost          =                 $80
profit        = 20% × $80 =      16
selling price =                 $96 (which is incorrect!)
```

But suppose the problem had stated that something cost you $100 and you sold it for $80. What was your percent of loss? In this instance, you lost $20 of the $100 ($100 − $80 = $20), and you want to know what part this $20 is of the $100. This can be shown as the fraction $20/$100, which can be converted to a percent:

$$\frac{\$20}{\$100} = .20 = 20\% \text{ loss}$$

It is very important that you determine the correct relationship(s) in any given problem. In the very first problem above, suppose you had been asked what percent your cost ($80) was of the selling price ($100). You want to know what part the cost is of the selling price. This can be expressed as follows:

$$\frac{\$80}{\$100} = .80 = 80\% \text{ (of the selling price)}$$

Or suppose you had been asked what part (percent) the selling price ($100) was of your cost ($80). Place the selling price over the cost as shown below:

$$\frac{\$100}{\$80} = 1.25 = 125\% \text{ (of the cost)}$$

As you can see, working with these situations involves setting up a relationship in the form of a fraction and then converting the resulting decimal to a percent.

Practice: You have an old ladder that is 20 feet long. You buy a new one that is 30 feet long. First, sketch below the two ladders.

a. How much longer, in percent, is the new ladder than the old
   ladder? _____%   2-43

b. What percent is the new ladder of the old ladder?
   _____%   2-44

c. What percent is the old ladder of the new ladder?
   _____%   2-45

d. How much shorter, in percent, is the old ladder than the
   new ladder? _____%   2-46

In this chapter, attention has been given to the explanation and general use of fractions, decimals and percents. In the following chapters, the focus will be on the explanation and use of the three as they specifically relate to the real estate business.

Chapter 3

Percent in Real Estate

KEY MATH TERMS

Percent: per hundred; per hundred parts

Percentage: a part of a whole; an amount

Formula: a rule or principle expressed in either words or symbols

Base: the total amount involved in a problem

Rate: a percent involved in a problem

Result: a part of the total amount involved in a problem

Memory Device: A mnemonic aid; intended to assist in remembering

In the real estate business, you cannot perform in a satisfactory manner unless you develop the ability to solve percent and percentage problems. This chapter will help you build those skills.

In many real estate problems, you may first have to convert fractions to decimals or percents or vice versa. It is easier to work a problem and you run less chance of making errors if you express numbers in the same form in the same problem.

Example: A property is sold for $96,000. The total sales commission is 7% and is divided as follows: the listing office will receive 5/10 of the sales commission, the selling office will receive 5/10 of the sales commission, and the salesperson will receive .60 of the selling office's commission. How much will the salesperson earn?

sale price × rate of commission = total sales commission
   $96,000 × .07 = $6,720
selling office's commission = .5 × $6,720 = $3,360
salesperson's commission = .60 × $3,360 = $2,016

The above illustration points to the fact that percents, decimals and fractions are all brothers and sisters with "hundreds" as common parents (for example, 6%, .06 and 6/100 all have a common reference source).

Percent and Percentage

Some people have difficulty with percents and percentages because the difference between percent and percentage has not been explained. The two are not the same, although both use hundreds as their source.

Percent is technically, and accurately, the Rate, that is, the fractional part of something. For example, the rate of taxation on a gallon of gasoline may be 9%. Rate is expressed as a percent.

Percentage is the actual amount (more and more frequently called a Result) obtained by applying the above-mentioned percent to a Base figure. For example, assume a rate of taxation on gas of 9%. Gas is selling for $1.10 per gallon, and you buy 10 gallons. The percentage would be the amount derived:

base price of gas	$ 1.10
number of gallons	× 10
total base cost of gas	$11.00
tax percent	× .09
percentage	$ .99 (the Result of multiplying total Base cost times Rate)

While closely related to each other, it is apparent that percent and percentage are different things. Their relationship may be taught by math teachers as follows:

Percent is a rate, so express percent as *Rate.*

Percentage is an amount, which is the *Result* of multiplying Base times Rate.

Base is the total amount involved in a problem.

Therefore, the formulas are:

Rate (percent) = Result ÷ Base
Result (percentage) = Base × Rate
Base (total amount) = Result ÷ Rate

Remembering the terms and their relationships is difficult for many persons. As a consequence, many people teaching and learning real estate math have sought other ways to express the above formulas. A memory device in the form of a common geometric figure is an aid used by many to remember how to solve almost any problem dealing with percents and percentages.

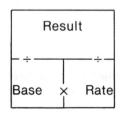 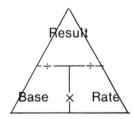 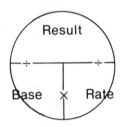

But notice that identical information and symbols appear in each. Because the geometric shape can be omitted without losing any of the value of the memory aid, from now on, this valuable device will simply be presented as an enlarged letter T with the appropriate math symbols included (see below).

Some call the use of the above figures the IRV system, indicating its use in solving Interest, Rate, and Value problems (see Chapter 7). This title, while accurate, is too restrictive, because this memory aid will assist you in solving a wide range of problems involving percents and percentages.

Use of the Memory Device

No one learns to play a piano or throw a football without practice. The same is true of real estate math. Working the suggested practice segments found throughout this book will develop skills and confidence. In the same way, practice with the following uses of the memory device will help you gain the proficiency you want and need.

Whether stated or unstated, all percent problems involve three variables (elements). Interest problems involve Time also. But the three variables common to all percent problems are:

        Rate (percent)

        Base (total amount)

        Result (percentage, a part of the total amount)

The elements necessary to solve percent problems are included in the memory aid, thereby assisting you to remember and use the three formulas shown earlier. To find the correct math operation to solve a problem involving percent, you need only check your memory aid, once you learn how to use it. Note that the horizontal line serves the same purpose as the horizontal line in a fraction—to indicate division.

At least two variables will be given to you in every percent problem. Sometimes they are "hidden." Careful analysis of the problem is necessary to identify correctly the variables given. Once variables are identified, place them in their appropriate places in the memory device. The missing variable, plus the operation that must be performed to find it, will become apparent.

First, sketch an enlarged letter T about the size of the one shown opposite.

Next, place the three mathematical signs in their proper locations as shown.

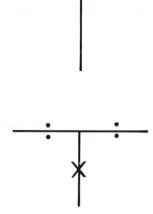

Finally, assign the three
    variables to their
    proper places
    around the T.

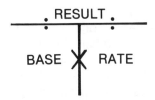

The number on top of the T is always divided by a bottom number; because the Base represents the total amount of something, the Base usually will be the largest number among the variables.

If the Rate is the missing (unknown) variable, place your thumb or finger over the place reserved around the T for Rate. The visible portion of the T memory aid that remains indicates that you must divide the percentage Result by the Base. If it is the percentage Result that is to be determined, cover the area of the T reserved for Result; the operation to perform is Base × Rate. Do not hesitate to sketch this little memory aid whenever solving percent problems.

Assume that your customer wants to buy a home costing $88,000 and that the best financing available requires a 15% down payment. How much is required as a down payment?

What is the total amount (Base)? $88,000

What is the percent (Rate) required for the down payment?   15%

What is the percentage (Result)? _____13,200 ?_____

Use of the memory aid reveals:

To find the answer, do as the memory aid
    indicates.

Multiply $88,000 times 15%.

To multiply, you must first change the 15% to its
    decimal form (.15).

The missing percentage, or Result, is found to
    be:

$88,000 × .15 = $13,200 (required as a down
    payment).

Mr. R. U. Shure received a notice from his mortgagee (lender) that last year his total interest paid on a $58,000 mortgage was $6,090. Mr. Shure would like to verify that he is not paying more interest than the mortgage agreement specifies. What interest rate is he paying?

Base (total of mortgage balance) $58,000
Result (percentage) $ 6,090
Rate (percent)   ?

The memory device shows:

$6,090 ÷ $58,000 = .105 or 10½% interest rate

Perhaps the most common use of the three variables is to find the Base because investors frequently use this method to determine the value of income-producing property.

Example: Mr. Lotsa Cash comes to you for help in finding a good investment in a relatively new apartment house. You do some investigating and find a property that nets approximately $24,000 annually with an asking price of $187,000. Mr. Cash informs you that he must have at least a 14% return on his money annually or he will not buy. Therefore, the $24,000 net income must be at least 14% of the sale price, whatever the amount. Will you advise him to acquire the property in question? Which of the variables do you have for use with the memory aid?

Result (percentage) $24,000
Rate (percent)   14%
Base (total amount)   ?

The $187,000 is the asking price, not the amount Mr. Cash must pay to get a 14% return. The Base is the unknown element:

$24,000 ÷ .14 = $171,428.57

Thus, the most that Mr. Cash should be advised to pay for the property is $171,400.

This same memory device can be used to find: (1) the assessed value if you have the property tax bill and the millage rate; (2) the actual interest rate charged by a department store if you know the finance charge on your monthly bill and the total amount of the bill; and (3) the amount of earned sales commission if the commission rate and sale price are known. A little experimentation will reveal an ever-expanding number of situations in which the memory aid can be used.

For example, 61,500 is 93% of what number? After reading the question, you realize that 61,500 is the percentage of some number, and the percent, or Rate, is 93%.

Using the T aid, the operation indicated is

61,500 ÷ .93 = 66,129.032 or
                      66,129 (rounded)

Or suppose that you made a 15% down payment on a tract of undeveloped land. The down payment amounted to $8,250. What was the purchase price?

Result (percentage) $8,250
Rate (percent)   15%
Base (total amount)   ?

$8,250 ÷ .15 = $55,000

It is quite possible to encounter a real estate situation in which a property owner has the information needed to establish a selling price but does not know how to use the information. Suppose you go to list a lakefront property. The owner tells you that five of her neighbors have sold within the past six months, and that the five sales showed, on the average, a property's original cost was 34% less than its current selling price. She says she paid $84,800 seven years ago.

With this information, you know that $84,800 is 34% less than some unknown total amount (property value, or Base). Notice that the problem states 34% less than, not 34% of, some unknown total amount. Using the 34% in the memory device will produce the wrong answer.

While the Base is unknown, you do know that the Base is the total amount of current value and can be represented by 100%. The known percentage amount ($84,800) can be represented by 100% minus 34% or 66%. Thus, $84,800 is 66% of some unknown amount.

Rate (percent)   66%
Result (percentage) $84,800
Base (total amount)   ?

$84,800 ÷ .66 = $128,484.84 or
                      $128,485 (rounded)

The previous problem clearly illustrates that while enough numbers may be given in a problem, they may not be ready to be inserted as is into the memory aid (or formula). Remember that percentage is an amount that represents, and can be represented by, a percent.

The following are just two of the many day-to-day questions that can be answered through the use of this memory device.

Practice: Your competitor sold a house for $89,800. The seller said that he paid a sales commission of $4,041. What sales commission rate did your competitor charge?

<u>   4 1/2 %   </u> 3-1

A client is considering the purchase of a commercial property for $1,522,500 cash. She will not buy unless a reasonable probability exists that the property will produce a 16% net return on investment. How much net income must the property produce to qualify for purchase?

<u>   243,600   </u> 3-2

The Five Steps in Percent Problems

The two situations above are common in real estate. To solve either of the problems, you must do exactly the same things that must be done in every case in which problems involving percent are encountered. There are <u>five</u> steps to take.

Step 1   You must read the problem carefully and analyze the situation, with the first objective being to determine which variable is missing.

Step 2   Reread the problem statement and label the available information as Rate (percent), Base (total amount), or Result (percentage). Simple drawings and arithmetic may need to be done before the labeling can be accomplished. This was illustrated earlier where the original property cost was 34% less than the current selling price. You had to find what percent of current market value was represented by a previous purchase price. The previous purchase price was 100% less 34% or 66% of today's value.

Step 3   Once all of the available information has been labeled, place each variable in the proper position within the memory aid.

Step 4   To solve the problem, find the missing variable by performing the math operation indicated by the two known variables.

Step 5   Check your answer: Substitute your answer in its proper place as one of the known variables, and pretend one of the other variables is the unknown.

This same procedure may be used for solving all percent problems, regardless of how long or involved they may be. You will find the use of this memory device helpful in dealing with net listings, sales commissions, depreciation, profit and loss rates, return on investment, tax problems based on percent of purchase price or appraised value, interest problems—in fact, in all situations involving percent.

Undoubtedly, you will find that you will not need the memory aid to help you in analyzing and solving all word problems. The important point to remember is that it is a visual representation of an equation. The number placed on the top of the T (the Result section) must be a result derived from multiplication of the two bottom section numbers (the Base and Rate sections).

Sometimes the information provided in a word problem is so abundant that you have difficulty identifying the data needed. Practice is the answer. Sometimes the information provided will not be in a form that fits into the memory device. The information must be converted to a form that can be used. Sketching pictures may help you.

Assume that an owner received a net of $67,200 from the sale of his home. The selling broker received a 7½% sales commission. What was the total sale price of the home?

It did not take you long to identify the missing variable—the Base (sale price) is missing. But when you try to use the information you placed in the memory aid, you discover that $67,200 cannot be the correct Result if 7½% is correct as the Rate. The Base would have to be an unbelievable $896,000 if both numerals were correct! You know that $67,200 is the net amount the seller actually received. You also know that 7½% was the commission rate. Aha! The 7½% relates to the commission, not to the net amount! You have to find the total sale price (the Base). If 7½% of the total sale price was paid as a commission, then the $67,200 is what was left of the total sale price, or 92½% (100%− 7½%). Placing 92½% in the Rate section of the memory aid and then performing the math operation indicated, the total sale price is found to be:

$$\$67,200 \div .925 = \$72,648.648 \text{ or}$$
$$\$72,650 \text{ (rounded)}$$

Memory Device Practice Problems

a. What is 18% of $29,000?

₱ 5220   3-3

b. 6,474 is what percent of 41,500?   _15.6%_ 3-4

c. 291 is 3% of what amount?   _9700_ 3-5

d. An apartment complex produces a 16% return on
    investment, amounting to $22,000 per year. What did
    the owner pay for the property?   _137,500_ 3-6

e. A house sold for $79,000. If the salesperson received
    $2,765 as a commission for selling the house, what
    percent of the sale price was her commission?   _3.1/2%_ 3-7

f. The purchase price on a property was $110,000. The
    brokerage firm selling the property received one-half of
    the total commission of 8%. How much did the selling
    firm receive?   _4400_ 3-8

Calculating Commissions

Assume that you have just concluded a net listing agreement for an estate. The owner has told you that he must have $435,000 net and has agreed that you can add your commission and legitimate expenses to his net amount to arrive at a sale price. Your knowledge of the law and local customs tells you that you are entitled to a 10% commission plus expenses. What will the amount of your sales commission be? Determine your answer before continuing. $_____

Did you write down $43,500? Wrong! A sales commission is based on the selling price. If you take $43,500 as your commission, you would be accepting 10% of the net listing price, not the 10% of the sale price to which you are entitled.

The solution involves careful analysis of the problem, and once again the memory device is of assistance. If you are allowed a 10% sales commission, then the net listing price of $435,000 represents 90% of the sale price, disregarding expenses, which will be added later. The correct way to find the sale price, before expenses, is to divide .90 into $435,000. By doing so, you are saying that $435,000 is 90% of some amount.

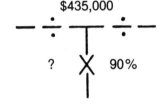

$435,000 ÷ .90 = $483,333.33 or
                   $483,333 (rounded)

Sale price before expenses	$483,333
Net amount required by owner	−435,000
Your 10% commission	$ 48,333
10% of $435,000 ("Wrong!")	− 43,500
Possible LOSS TO YOU if not computed correctly!	$ 4,833!

You now add the estimated expenses to the initial sale price of $483,333 to determine the total sale price. If all of the estimated expenses are not required, the difference would be returned to the owner.

The point of the above illustration is to demonstrate the importance to you of knowing how to use percents and decimals correctly.

Many brokers use various production plateaus as the criterion for increasing their salespersons' commissions. For instance, a salesperson may be paid 50% of the broker's commission up to a total production plateau of $200,000 of property sold by the salesperson. From $200,001 to $350,000, the salesperson's share may be increased to 55% of the broker's commission. And there may be further plateaus.

Suppose the broker's listing agreement specified that a 7% sales commission was to be paid on the sale price of a parcel. Then assume that a salesperson who has passed the $200,000 plateau sold a property listed by the salesperson's broker. The salesperson received 55% of the 7% sales commission. Disregarding listing commissions and Multiple Listing Service (MLS) fees, how much did the salesperson earn if he or she sold the property for $84,000?

Do you see the similarity between the previous paragraphs and the memory device practice problems? After rereading the stated conditions and properly identifying the information provided in the problem:

First, find the total sales commission:

Rate	7%
Base	$84,000
Result	?

$84,000 × .07 = $5,880 (total sales commission)

Second, find the salesman's commission:

Rate	55%
Base	$5,880
Result	?

$5,880 × .55 = $3,234 (salesman's commission)

Once you are confident of the correct procedure to follow, there is no need to employ the memory device as an aid. However, do not hesitate to rely on it when in the process of analyzing a word problem or to use it to assist in labeling information provided.

Often a broker who lists a property with higher-than-normal value will agree to a graduated sales commission. This provides an incentive for the broker to get the seller the very best price possible.

For example, suppose a broker lists a relatively new office building for sale. He agrees to accept a 5% sales commission on the first $200,000 of the actual sale price, 7½% on the next $500,000, 8½% on the next $500,000, and 10% of anything greater (over $1,200,000, in other words). What would the broker's total sales commission amount to if he sold the office building for $2,200,000?

The solving of this problem is best shown through a step-by-step procedure, as follows:

Step 1
```
  $200,000 = first increment of sale price
×      .05 = first increment of commission
$10,000.00 = total first increment commission
```

Step 2
```
  $500,000 = second increment of sale price
×      .075 = second increment of commission
$37,500.00 = total second increment commission
```

Step 3
```
  $500,000 = third increment of sale price
×      .085 = third increment of commission
$42,500.00 = total third increment commission
```

Step 4 $200,000 = first increment of sale price
       500,000 = second increment of sale price
    + 500,000 = third increment of sale price
  $1,200,000 = total of first three increments

Step 5 $2,200,000 = total sale price
  − 1,200,000 = total of first three increments
  $1,000,000 = amount to which 10% sales commission is applied

Step 6 $1,000,000 = last increment of sale price
  ×   .10 = last increment of commission
    $100,000 = total last increment commission

Step 7 $10,000 = first increment commission
    37,500 = second increment commission
    42,500 = third increment commission
  + 100,000 = last increment commission
  $190,000 = total sales commission!!!

Suppose the salesperson who actually negotiated the transaction had been promised 63% of the total sales commission. How much would be earned?

    $190,000 = total sales commission
  ×   .63 = salesperson's portion of commission
    $119,700 = amount earned by salesperson!!!

Practice Commission Problems

a. A building is sold for $160,000. The broker agreed to accept a commission of 7½% on the first $100,000 of the purchase price and a smaller percent on anything over $100,000. If the total sales commission is $11,100, what is the smaller rate of commission the broker has also agreed to accept?

_____ 3-9

b. You have sold a small warehouse for $97,500. Your employment contract specifies that you will receive 50% of the total sales commission for properties you sell. If the rate of commission is 10%, what amount will you receive?

_____ 3-10

c. The office where you work charges a 7% sales commission and pays salespeople 14% of sales commission on all residential listings. The remainder of the sales commission is equally divided between the broker and the salesperson who makes the sale. If you list and sell a property for $75,500, what amount will you receive?

_____ 3-11

Calculate the missing element for each of the five sales:

	Selling Price	Commission Rate	Commission Earned	
d.	$169,000	5%	$8,450	3-12
e.	$80,750	7½%	6056.25	3-13
f.	89,060	6%	$5,340	3-14
g.	$77,779	7%	5444.53	3-15
h.	$98,000	7.75%	$7,595	3-16

Chapter 4

Mortgage Math

The vast majority of all real estate transactions involve the use of mortgage loans because buyers are seldom able to purchase a home by paying for it in cash. This loaning/ borrowing of money has prompted the creation of special words related to this activity:

Principal (P): the amount of money borrowed
Interest (I): the cost of using someone else's money
Rate of interest (R): the annual percent that must be paid to use the money
Time (T): the term or duration a borrower has use of money

When any three of these elements in a mortgage problem are known, the fourth element can always be calculated. The following formulas apply:

$$I = PRT \qquad P = \frac{I}{RT} \qquad R = \frac{I}{PT} \qquad T = \frac{I}{PR}$$

All of these formulas will be incorporated into the memory device, as explained later in this chapter.

CALCULATING INTEREST

Most people would not stop to figure the actual rate of interest if offered a loan of $100 at a cost of $1 per week. Yet, over a period of one year, this would mean paying $52 in interest, which is a 52% annual rate of interest! If the interest were $1 per month, the annual rate would be 12%.

While interest is usually charged monthly, interest rates are normally expressed as a yearly (annual) rate. When dealing with interest problems involving one year only, the calculation of interest is especially easy ($I = P \times R \times T$). For example, what is the interest on $10,000 at 8% per year for 1 year?

Interest = Principal $\times$ Rate $\times$ Time
= $10,000 $\times$ 8% per year $\times$ 1 year
= $10,000 $\times$ .08
= $800

In dealing with Time, all calculations are related to a one-year period.

> To find annual interest: principal × rate
> To find monthly interest: annual interest ÷ 12
> To find daily interest: annual interest ÷ 365; or monthly interest ÷ the number of days in the month of concern

Answers will be more accurate if figures are carried out at least three places to the right of the decimal point and kept at least three decimal places until the final answer. In the final answer, round off to two decimal places.

Example: What amount of interest must be paid on $10,000 at 9½% for 4 months and 7 days?

> Annual interest   = $10,000 × .095 = $950
> Monthly interest = $950 ÷ 12 = $79.167
> Daily interest   = $950 ÷ 365 = $2.603
>
> 4 months = 4 × $79.167 = $316.668
> 7 days   = 7 × $2.603 = +   18.221
> $334.889 or
> $334.89 (rounded)

Using Time in the Memory Device

Interest is always the Result of a borrowed amount (principal) multiplied by a Rate of interest multiplied by a period of Time. The first three terms—interest (Result), principal (Base) and rate of interest (Rate)—fit easily into the memory aid. However, to solve mortgage problems, the aid must be modified to include the fourth term—Time—which is a very important factor in money lending:

The amount of interest should always be placed over the horizontal line of the memory device. Because interest is a form of income, when a problem does not mention interest but does refer to income, then the amount of income should be placed above the horizontal line of the T.

In these four-element problems, perform the multiplication first, then the division. (In any equation in which parentheses appear, first perform the math operation within the parentheses.)

Example: What is the principal amount borrowed if a 9% rate of interest results in payment of $135 interest for a period of 6 months?

$$\text{Principal} = \$135 \div (9\% \times 6 \text{ months})$$
$$= \$135 \div (.09 \times .5)$$
$$= \$135 \div .045$$
$$= \$3,000$$

Note: Time must be expressed in years, or portions of years, because interest rates are understood to be annual rates (unless otherwise indicated).

Example: How long did a borrower have use of $42,000 if a 9½% rate of interest cost her $9,975?

$$\text{Time} = \$9,975 \div (\$42,000 \times 9\frac{1}{2}\%)$$
$$= \$9,975 \div (\$42,000 \times .095)$$
$$= \$9,975 \div \$3,990$$
$$= 2.5 \text{ years, or } 2\frac{1}{2} \text{ years}$$

Suppose she had paid only $997.50 in interest with the same borrowed amount and interest rate as above. How long would she have had the use of the loan?

$$\text{Time} = \$997.50 \div (\$42,000 \times .095)$$
$$= \$997.50 \div \$3,990$$
$$= .25 \text{ years, or } 3 \text{ months}$$

Practice Interest Problems

a. On a $3,000 loan for 6 months, $146.25 was paid as interest. What was the rate of interest?

_____ 4-1

b. What is the interest on a $68,000 mortgage at 11.6% rate of interest for 9 months?

_____ 4-2

c. On a $2,000 loan with a 9% interest rate, $60 interest was paid. How long was the term of the loan?

_____ 4-3

A MORTGAGE FINANCIAL PACKAGE

A mortgage financial package includes the computation of: (1) the down payment; (2) the loan amount; (3) the discount point impact; (4) the taxes on the mortgage, where applicable and; (5) the total monthly payment, to include principal, interest, taxes and insurance. In some instances, the broker or salesperson may need to prepare a financial package comparing figures for several loan plans, including fixed-rate and adjustable-rate mortgages.

Computing the Down Payment

The minimum down payment required will depend on the type of financing arranged—FHA, VA or conventional mortgage loan.

FHA Minimum Down Payments ("Required Investment")—203(b) Program

The lesser of Appraised Value plus HUD-Approved Closing Costs or Total Acquisition Cost	Down Payment ("Required Investment")
$50,000 or less	3%
More than $50,000	3% of the first $25,000 plus 5% of any amount over $25,000*

Examples (assume a maximum FHA-insured loan amount of $77,900 applies):

	Appraised Value Plus Closing Costs		Rate Schedule		Down Payment (Req. Invest.)	Loan Amount Required*
#1	$49,900	×	3%	=	$1,497	$48,403
#2	$81,300					
	First $25,000	×	3%	=	$ 750	
	Remaining $56,300	×	5%	=	+2,815	
					$ 3,565	$77,735

When the appraised value plus closing costs (or total acquisition cost) is *greater than $50,000*, there is a shortcut method that can be used to calculate the required FHA down payment: multiply the total acquisition cost by 5% and subtract $500. ($81,300 × .05 = $4,065 − $500 = $3,565 down payment)

---

* If the calculated loan amount exceeds the applicable maximum FHA-insured loan amount, then the maximum FHA loan amount is subtracted from the lesser of the appraised value plus closing costs or the total acquisition cost to determine the down payment. Maximum FHA-insurable loan amounts vary from area to area. They are set by the various HUD regional offices based on the median price of new housing in the local area. At this writing, for example, the maximum FHA-insurable loan amounts for single-family dwellings throughout the U.S. ranged from $67,500 to $124,875. Contact the HUD regional office in your area for the current FHA maximum loan limits that apply.

Practice Problems Calculating FHA Down Payments (assume that $88,350 is the maximum FHA-insured loan amount):

	Appraised Value & Closing Costs	Down Payment	
a.	$44,500	_____	4-4
b.	$61,700	_____	4-5
c.	$72,400	_____	4-6
d.	$92,000	_____	4-7
e.	$116,000	_____	4-8

Note: In this book, the focus is on developing math abilities and confidence. However, in actual practice, all FHA-insured loans are made in $50 increments. FHA-insured loans are rounded *down* to the next $50 increment. This practice increases the down payment by the amount rounded down. Example #1 on the opposite page resulted in a minimum down payment of $1,497. Subtract from the total cost of $49,900 the $1,497 down payment, and the loan amount is $48,403, which is not an even multiple of $50. FHA rounds the maximum loan amount down to the nearest $50, so the FHA-insured loan in this instance would be $48,400, and the adjusted down payment would be $1,500.

VA Minimum Down Payments

Federal law does not currently require a down payment to be made by qualified veterans. The requirement for a down payment is normally left to the discretion of participating lenders. Many lenders will accept VA guarantees in lieu of cash down payments, allowing eligible veterans to buy a home without a down payment. (When a manufactured home is involved, however, a down payment of at least 5% is required.) VA does require a "funding fee" or "user's fee"; the fee varies with the size of the down payment (the larger the down payment, the smaller the fee). It may be added to the loan amount or paid at closing; and it is a percent of the mortgage amount (but it may be waived entirely for service-disabled veterans and surviving spouses).

Conventional Loan Down Payments

Conventional mortgage loans vary from 70% to 95% of total value. Private mortgage insurance (PMI) arrangements may permit a buyer to pay as little as 5% of the appraised value as a down payment. However, conventional mortgages normally require a larger down payment than government-sponsored loans.

Whatever the percent of selling price required as a down payment, correct use of the memory aid will always show the operation needed to find the amount of down payment required for a conventional loan.

Selling price	= Base
Percent required as down payment	= Rate
Amount of down payment	= Result

Down payment = selling price × percent required

Example: What is the down payment for a house appraised at $84,000 and requiring a 20% down payment?

$84,000 × .20 = $16,800

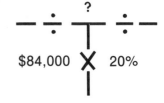

Practice Problems Calculating Conventional Loan Down Payments

a. You are a broker and have placed in escrow a 10% earnest money deposit on the appraised value of a house. A mortgage company has agreed to lend the buyer $58,800, which is 80% of the appraised value of the property. How much earnest money do you have in escrow?

_____ 4-9

b. A buyer has made an earnest money deposit of $5,000 on a home selling for $79,500. A bank has agreed to lend the buyer 75% of the sale price. How much more cash must the buyer furnish to complete the total required down payment?

_____ 4-10

c. A house is selling for $89,700. A savings and loan association will finance 90% of the purchase price. How much will the buyer be required to pay as a down payment?

_____ 4-11

d. A buyer has agreed to pay 10% down on a home selling for $71,500. A mortgage has been arranged for the balance of the purchase price. The buyer has agreed to pay 1½% of the loan amount at closing for prepaid private mortgage insurance. How much money must the buyer bring to the closing if he has already deposited $1,000 with the seller?

_____ 4-12

Computing Mortgage Loan Amounts

All FHA, VA and conventional mortgage loans are based on appraisals of the property that is offered as security. Once the appraised value of the property is determined by a competent appraiser, it is used to assist the lender in calculating the maximum amount of the loan.

FHA Loans—Regular FHA 203(b) Program

The guidelines for making FHA loans were mentioned in the section on down payments. Regular FHA loans (the 203(b) program) are restricted to the following maximums:

If either the appraised value plus closing costs or the total acquisition cost is *$50,000 or less*, 97% of the appraised value plus closing costs or the total acquisition cost, whichever is less, will be insured.

If both the appraised value plus closing costs and the total acquisition cost are *more than $50,000*, the following applies:

97% of the first $25,000 *plus*
95% of the balance of the appraised value (including closing
        costs) or the total acquisition cost, whichever is less.

For properties over $50,000, the combination of the above two increments may not exceed the maximum FHA-established insured-loan amount for the area in which the property is located.

Example: Assume that a buyer wants to purchase a home appraised at $72,500 and the closing costs are estimated to be $2,100. Determine the FHA loan amount.

Acquisition cost   = $72,500 + $2,100 = $74,600
97% × first $25,000   = $24,250
95% × remaining $49,600 = <u>47,120</u>
        calculated loan amount = $71,370

(While the loan amount of $71,370 would, in actual practice, be adjusted down to $71,350, for mathematical accuracy in this book the loan amount will not be adjusted.)

Example: The appraised value plus HUD-approved closing costs is $98,000 for a property in an area where the maximum FHA-insured loan amount is $82,800. The loan amount and down payment would be:

$98,000
less <u>25,000</u> × 97% = $24,250
$73,000 × 95% = <u>69,350</u>
$93,600 (exceeds loan limit)

When the calculated loan amount exceeds the maximum FHA-insured loan amount, the loan amount is the maximum FHA-insured loan amount for the area. The required down payment is the difference between the appraised value plus closing costs and the maximum FHA-insured loan amount.

$98,000 appraised value plus closing costs
<u>− 82,800</u> maximum FHA-insured loan amount
$15,200 required down payment

VA Loans

The law permits lenders to lend 100% of reasonable property value to a veteran. Before the loan can be made, a VA-approved appraiser must appraise the property to establish a reasonable value. No formula exists for calculating VA loan amounts because lenders are allowed to exercise their own discretion in establishing the percent of property value they will lend. At this writing, the generally accepted maximum VA loan amount without a down payment is $144,000. However, for mortgages that exceed $144,000, VA will guarantee to a lender 25% of the VA loan up to a maximum guarantee of $46,000, in effect creating a loan limit of $184,000 (four times the current maximum guarantee).

Conventional Loans

As indicated earlier, lenders making conventional loans may now lend up to 95% of the appraised value if private mortgage insurance is purchased. The maximum amount of a conventional loan available will, therefore, vary from 70% to 95% of the appraised value. A survey of local lenders will disclose the maximum loan available.

Example: How much money will a lender loan if a property has been appraised at $104,500 and the buyer/borrower is required to invest 20% of the property value?

Appraised Value − Required Investment = Available Loan
         100%   −   20%   =   80%
$104,500 × .80 = $83,600 available loan

Practice: The newspaper advertises a condominium selling for $69,700 with 95% financing and no closing costs. How much mortgage will the buyer be allowed if the minimum down payment is made?

_____ 4-13

Mortgage Discount Points

For years, extra charges called mortgage discount points were necessary to make the lower interest rates of federally sponsored mortgages competitive with the higher interest rates of conventional mortgage loans. As the money market has reacted to increased demand, inflation and a reduced supply of money, the character of discount points has changed. Lenders now charge points as an interest "rate adjustment factor." In other words, to increase the "real yield" from a mortgage without showing an increase in the interest rate on the mortgage, a charge is levied. These discount points are based on the loan amount, not the selling price. With conventional and FHA loans, the borrower normally pays the discount points. With VA loans, the borrower is prohibited from paying the discount points but will be required to pay a funding or user's fee (mentioned earlier).

Lenders use either prepared tables or a rule of thumb to determine the number of discount points that must be paid. Each discount point will increase the real yield from a loan by 1/8 of 1% (1 point = 1/8%). Therefore, for each discount point charged by a lender, add 1/8% to the mortgage interest rate to determine the lender's real yield from the loan.

Note: This calculation is designed to find the real or effective mortgage interest rate expressed as an _annual percent_, not as a dollar amount. The contract interest rate will not change as such.

But to determine the actual cost, in dollars, added by discount points, each discount point is equal to 1% of the mortgage balance (1 point = 1%). The mortgage balance (loan amount) is multiplied by this discount percent to find the dollar amount of the discount being charged.

Example: Assume the market rate of interest is 10¼% and the FHA rate of interest is 9½%. The following steps should be used to determine: (a) the discount points required to equal the market rate of interest and (b) the amount of discount charged on a $60,000 FHA mortgage:

a. Discount points required to equal the market rate:
   1. Calculate the difference in the two rates:
      current market rate − government interest rate = difference
      10¼% − 9½% = 3/4%
   2. Convert the difference to eighths of a percent:
      3/4% = 6/8%
   3. Convert the eighths to discount points (1/8% = 1 point):
      6/8% ÷ 1/8% per point = 6 discount points

b. Amount of discount charged:
   1. Convert discount points to discount rate (1 point = 1%):
      6 points × 1% per point = 6%
   2. Calculate the amount of discount:
      total loan amount × discount rate = amount of discount
      $60,000 × .06 = $3,600 (cost of discount points)

With most loans, a borrower usually does not know about all of the above information. The more common experience is for the borrower or his agent to be told that a loan will require payment of 4 discount points, or 3, or 5, or whatever. The problem then is not only to calculate the amount of discount cost (step "b" above) but also to determine the real yield to the lender.

Using the same situation as above, assume that the need is to find the amount of real yield to the lender if 6 discount points are charged for an FHA loan showing a "contract rate" of 9½% interest.

convert discount points to percent of increase:
(1 point = 1/8 of 1% increase)
6 points × 1/8% per point = 6/8% increase
add to the contract rate the percent of increase:
9½% + 6/8% = 10¼% (real yield to lender)

When solving mortgage discount problems, remember that the cost of discount points is figured on the amount of the loan (1 discount point = 1% of the loan amount).

Practice Problems—Discount Points

a. A bank has agreed to lend $87,900 at 10½% for 30 years. The borrower is to pay 2 discount points. How much will the borrower be required to pay?

_____ 4-14

b. What will the real yield be to the bank in the above problem?

_____ 4-15

c. FHA has agreed to insure a loan for the purchase of a new home selling for $77,500, which includes closing costs. An approved savings and loan association will make the actual loan at 9% interest rate, but the borrower is to pay 4 discount points.

How much will the discount points cost the borrower?   _____ 4-16

What will the real yield be to the lender?   _____ 4-17

d. A lender requires a real yield of 10.25% to make a loan. VA interest rates have an imposed ceiling of 9.5%. How many points must the lender charge to obtain the required real yield?

_____ 4-18

e. A builder has an FHA loan commitment of $63,000 on a house he is building. He has been told by a bank willing to lend the $63,000 that 3 discount points will be charged when the house is financed. The builder decides to be safe and adds the equivalent of 4 points to the price of the house. How much did the 4 points increase the cost of the house over the loan commitment amount?

_____ 4-19

Computing Taxes on Mortgages

Most states have enacted laws that levy taxes on all forms of debt instruments, including promissory notes, mortgages, deeds of trust, and other documents that create a legal debt and obligation to pay. For example, in many states, two separate taxes must be paid each time a *new* mortgage is created.

1. A state intangible tax on all new mortgages. This is a one-time tax and is not paid annually. For instance, the tax rate may be $.002 (two mills) per dollar of new indebtedness.

2. A state documentary stamp tax on the note that is part of the mortgage package. For instance, the tax rate may be $.32 per $100, or fractional part thereof, and is calculated on the face value of the note. This tax is a one-time tax paid when a new mortgage or loan document is created.

In states that levy taxes on new mortgages, every real estate transaction that is not an all-cash transaction will reflect the cost of these taxes on closing statements. Most states construct license examinations to require demonstration of an ability to compute the amount of taxes on new mortgages.

Example: Mr. Polk bought a home from Mr. and Mrs. Dade for $79,500. The sales contract acknowledged receipt of a $3,800 earnest money deposit and specified that Mr. Polk was to assume a $32,075 existing mortgage while the Dades were to take back a second mortgage in the amount of $30,000 in lieu of cash. Mr. Polk agreed to pay the balance of the purchase price in cash at closing. Using the above tax rates, what taxes would Mr. Polk pay if he has agreed to pay for any expense caused by the $30,000 loan?

Intangible tax on the new mortgage:

$30,000 loan amount $\times$ $.002 tax rate = $60

Documentary stamp tax on the note:

$30,000 $\div$ $100 increments = 300 taxable increments
300 taxable increments $\times$ $.32 tax rate = $96

Thus, the total taxes to be paid on the new loan are
$60 + $96 = $156

Example: Mr. Dunn bought a condominium for $69,575. He paid an earnest money deposit of $2,000 and assumed an existing mortgage of $43,250; the seller took back a second mortgage in the amount of $24,325 in lieu of cash. What taxes on the new mortgages would Mr. Dunn pay if he contracted to pay all taxes created by the new loan? Assume that the state levies taxes at the rates previously cited.

Intangible tax on mortgage:
  $24,325 × $.002 = $48.65
Documentary stamp tax on the note:
  $24,325 ÷ $100 = 243.25 taxable increments
    (.25 part requires the same tax as a whole increment; change
    fractional part to 1 whole increment)
  243 + 1 = 244 taxable increments
  244 taxable increments × $.32 = $78.08
Total taxes on new loan = $48.65 + $78.08 = $126.73

Practice: Compute the taxes required in the following situations, using the tax rates cited previously:

	New Mortgage Amount	Mortgage: Intangible Tax	Note: Doc. Stamp Tax	
a.	$48,000	_____	_____	4-20
b.	$87,000	_____	_____	4-21
c.	$56,850	_____	_____	4-22
d.	$92,760	_____	_____	4-23
e.	$126,420	_____	_____	4-24

Computing Monthly Payments

The computation of a level monthly payment necessary to pay both principal and interest for various rates of percent and loan amounts is done by computers. The results are a series of loan tables published in book and booklet form. Most banks, loan companies, and savings and loan associations have these loan table booklets available for brokers and sales-persons. Thus, you will not have to compute the monthly payments necessary to retire a loan over a period of time. However, you will need to know: (1) how to add property tax and hazard insurance costs to monthly mortgage payments to determine the total monthly payment to be paid to a lender and (2) how to allocate correct portions of the monthly payment to interest and to payment on borrowed principal.

Adding Taxes and Insurance to Monthly Payment

The correct procedure for dealing with property taxes and hazard insurance is to begin with the level monthly mortgage payment (principal and interest) obtained from a loan table. To this amount is added 1/12 of annual property taxes and 1/12 of the annual hazard insurance premium. Together, these four items are referred to as a PITI payment (principal, interest, taxes and insurance).

Example: A couple makes a monthly mortgage payment of $319.27 for principal and interest. Their annual property taxes are $784.20 and their homeowner's insurance is $192 per year. What are their total monthly PITI payments?

$784.20 ÷ 12 months = $65.35 per month for taxes
$192 ÷ 12 months   = $16.00 per month for insurance
total monthly payments = $319.27 + $65.35 + $16
                       = $400.62

Practice: A homeowner makes a monthly mortgage payment of $420.20 for principal and interest. Property taxes are $840 per year, and annual hazard insurance is $180. What is the total monthly PITI payment?

_____ 4-25

MORTGAGE AMORTIZATION

Mortgages on residential properties usually call for regular, equal payments (level-payment plan) that will include both interest payments and payments on the unpaid balance of the debt (principal). The amount of the payment that goes for interest gradually decreases, whereas the amount assigned to amortizing the debt (principal) gradually increases over the life of the mortgage. "Amortize" means to "kill" a mortgage through regular payments over time.

To calculate how much money is to be regarded as interest and how much is to be paid on the principal, only three facts are needed in this type of problem:

1. The outstanding amount of the debt (principal)

2. The rate of interest

3. The amount of the payment per period (usually monthly)

Difficulty in solving amortized mortgage problems usually occurs when no system is used. The following system, or procedure, is easy to use and will help reduce the chance of error. When amortizing a mortgage, sketch the following column headings on a piece of paper:

	Interest	Principal	New Balance
First month	_____	_____	_____
Second month	_____	_____	_____
Third month	_____	_____	_____

(and so on)

By arranging the format as above, the required steps to solve an amortization problem will become apparent. The format requires the first month's interest to be the initial entry in the table. Once the first month's interest has been computed and entered, the next two column headings, Principal and New Balance, indicate the next pieces of information needed.

Before going through an example, it is important to note the relationship of the following four steps for amortizing mortgages to the above format:

1. Principal Balance $\times$ Interest Rate = Annual Interest

2. Annual Interest $\div$ 12 months = first month's interest (place under Interest in table)

3. Monthly Mortgage Payment $-$ first month's interest = payment on principal balance (place under Principal)

4. Beginning Principal Balance $-$ principal payment = New Unpaid Principal Balance (place under New Balance and use to compute annual interest, if required). Repeat the above steps as many times as are required.

Example: You sell a home with a mortgage of $45,000 at 11½% interest. The prospect wants you to explain how much of his monthly payment will go for interest and how much will go for principal during the first three months. His monthly payment is $445.64.

Step 1
$45,000 = unpaid balance
× .115 = annual rate of interest
$5,175.00 = interest as if paid annually

Step 2
$431.25 = first month's interest (enter under Interest)
12 $5,175.00

Step 3
$445.64 = monthly payment
− 431.25 = interest for first month
$ 14.39 = payment on principal (enter under Principal)

But the prospect wanted to know about the first three months. So, you take credit for the $14.39 paid on the principal by subtracting that amount from the $45,000 beginning mortgage.

Step 4
$45,000.00 = principal
− 14.39 = principal paid the first month
$44,985.61 = unpaid balance (enter under New Balance)

Now repeat steps 1 through 4 to determine the answers for the second and third months.

Step 5
$44,985.61 = unpaid balance
× .115 = annual interest rate
$5,173.3451 = interest as if paid annually

Step 6
$ 431.1121 = second month's interest (round to $431.11 and enter
12 $5,173.3451   under Interest)

Step 7
$445.64 = monthly payment
− 431.11 = second month's interest
$ 14.53 = second month's principal (enter under Principal)

Step 8
$44,985.61 = unpaid balance
− 14.53 = second month's principal
$44,971.08 = new unpaid balance (enter under New Balance)

Step 9
$44,971.08 = new unpaid balance
× .115 = annual interest rate
$5,171.6742 = interest as if paid annually

Step 10
$430.9729 = third month's interest (round to $430.97 and enter
12 $5,171.6742   under Interest)

Step 11
$445.64 = monthly payment
− 430.97 = third month's interest
$ 14.67 = third month's principal (enter under Principal)

Thus, the answer to your prospect's question is:

	Interest	**Principal**
first month	$431.25	$14.39
second month	$431.11	$14.53
third month	$430.97	$14.67

Practice: Mr. and Mrs. Lovejoy have obtained a mortgage loan of $75,000 at 11¼%. The loan will be amortized by equal monthly payments of $728.45 over a period of 30 years. The monthly payment includes both principal and interest. What portion of the third month's payment will be paid on the loan principal?

_____ 4-26

Amortization over Extended Periods

Frequently, it becomes necessary to calculate the amount of interest paid over an extended period of time. For example, suppose a customer has been making a monthly payment on his mortgage for 14 years and is informed by the mortgagee (lender) that 22% of the mortgage has been paid. He asks you to calculate the total amount of interest he has paid on the loan during the 14 years he has been making payments.

You know that payments have been made for 14 years. You also know that 168 payments have been made (12 months × 14 years = 168 monthly payments). Multiply the total number of monthly payments made times the amount of the monthly payment required in the mortgage agreement to determine the total amount paid during the 14-year period. From this total amount paid, subtract the amount which has been paid on the mortgage (22% of the original loan amount). The difference is interest.

Example: You have paid $465.12 on your mortgage each month for 10 years. You learn that your mortgage is 17% paid off after 10 years. If the original amount borrowed was $53,900, how much total interest have you paid to date?

Step 1

$$
\begin{array}{r}
12 \\
\times\ 10 \\
\hline
120
\end{array}
$$
= months in a year
= years paid on mortgage
= months paid on mortgage to date

Step 2

$$
\begin{array}{r}
\$465.12 \\
\times\ 120 \\
\hline
\$55,814.40
\end{array}
$$
= monthly mortgage payment
= months paid on mortgage to date
= total amount paid to date

Step 3

$$
\begin{array}{r}
\$53,900 \\
\times\ .17 \\
\hline
\$9,163.00
\end{array}
$$
= amount originally borrowed
= percent of loan repaid to date
= principal repaid on loan to date

Step 4

$$
\begin{array}{r}
\$55,814.40 \\
-\ 9,163.00 \\
\hline
\$46,651.40
\end{array}
$$
= total amount paid to date
= principal repaid on loan to date
= total interest paid to date

Example: Assume that you pay on the mortgage in the above example throughout the entire 30-year period and pay it off completely. How much additional interest will be paid during the last 20 years of the mortgage?

Step 1
$$
\begin{array}{r}
12 = \text{months in a year} \\
\times\ 30 = \text{years paid on mortgage} \\
\hline
360 = \text{months paid on mortgage}
\end{array}
$$

Step 2
$$
\begin{array}{r}
\$465.12 = \text{monthly mortgage payment} \\
\times\ 360 = \text{months paid on mortgage} \\
\hline
\$167{,}443.20 = \text{total amount paid}
\end{array}
$$

Step 3
$$
\begin{array}{r}
\$167{,}443.20 = \text{total amount paid} \\
-\ 53{,}900.00 = \text{amount originally borrowed} \\
\hline
\$113{,}543.20 = \text{total interest paid}
\end{array}
$$

But the question asks how much additional interest was paid during the last 20 years.

Step 4
$$
\begin{array}{r}
\$113{,}543.20 = \text{total interest paid} \\
-\ 46{,}651.40 = \text{interest paid over first 10 years} \\
\hline
\$66{,}891.80 = \text{additional interest paid during the last 20 years}
\end{array}
$$

Practice: Mrs. South is thinking of selling her home. She obtains the following information from the bank financing her home. Over a period of 9 years, Mrs. South has paid off 12% of her mortgage. The original mortgage was $42,000 at 11% for 30 years. Her payments for principal and interest have been $399.98 per month.

a. How much interest has Mrs. South paid on her mortgage during the 9 years?

_____ 4-27

b. How much total interest will Mrs. South pay if she continues making payments over the full 30-year period?

_____ 4-28

REVIEW PROBLEMS

1. A nonamortized loan of $5,000 was made, payable in 18 months, with interest at 11%. What amount of interest will be collected at payment?

   _____

2. A contractor borrowed $74,000 at 12% interest to build a house. He paid the loan plus interest at the end of 6 months. How much interest did he pay?

   _____

3. A golf pro borrowed $15,000 at 10% interest to use as financing on the professional golf tour. At the end of the tour, he paid back his loan plus $1,125 in interest. How long did he use the money?

   _____

4. How much money must a banker lend at 11% in order to earn $33,000 interest in one year?

   _____

5. How much principal must be loaned to earn $24,000 in 6 months at 12% interest?

   _____

6. Mr. North paid $5,940 interest when he repaid the $54,000 he had borrowed at 11% interest to purchase an orange grove. How long did he have use of the money?

   _____

If FHA financing is used to buy a home (maximum loan amount = $88,350), what is the minimum down payment required for a home with an appraised value plus closing costs of:

7. $47,500   down payment = _____

8. $77,900   down payment = _____

9. $88,350   down payment = _____

10. A savings and loan association will finance your customer's home if an increase in actual yield of 1/2 of 1% in interest can be arranged. How many discount points must be charged?

_____

11. In an area in which the maximum FHA-insured loan amount is $124,875, FHA mortgages are going at 94 (this means FHA mortgages must be discounted 6%, or 6 points are charged to make a loan). How much will the discount points cost if a house's appraised value plus closing costs is $117,375 and FHA financing is used? (Round your answer to the nearest dollar.)

_____

12. A farm was sold for $165,000. The seller offered to permit the buyer to assume an existing mortgage of $88,000 if the buyer paid $50,000 as a down payment. The buyer preferred to refinance. He arranged to pay $30,000 down in cash and obtained a new loan for the remainder of the $165,000. What were the taxes on the new financing? (See page 52 for tax rates.)

_____

_____

13. A mortgage loan of $108,000 is amortized by payments of $947.79, including principal and interest (10%). How much of the second month's mortgage payment was paid on the principal?

_____

14. A house was sold under the following conditions:

purchase price	$85,750
down payment	$ 8,000
existing VA mortgage	$57,625
new second mortgage	$20,125

What is the total amount of mortgage-related taxes to be paid on the financing?

_____

15. Mary Perez pays $396.12 each month for principal and interest on her FHA mortgage. Her property taxes are $942 per year and her homeowner's insurance amounts to $168 per year. What is Ms. Perez's total monthly payment?

_____

16. Mr. Hecht has been paying on his home mortgage for 7 years. His monthly payments are $510.01 on an original loan of $51,500 at 11½% interest for 30 years. During the 7 years of payments, Mr. Hecht has paid off 12% of his original loan. How much interest has he paid in the 7 years?

_____

17. From the information in problem 16 above, how much interest will Mr. Hecht pay during the full 30-year term?

_____

Chapter 5

Real Estate Taxes

Property taxes are most commonly levied on an "ad valorem" basis, which means that real property is taxed "according to the value." However, the word "value" may mean assessed value, market value or taxable value, and each may represent a different amount.

In many states, the *assessed value* is a stated percent of current market value. For example, all homes may be assessed at 80% of market value. In other states, the assessed value is supposed to approximate full *market value* (exchange value).

Taxable value is determined by beginning with assessed value and subtracting any exemptions from taxation.

Example: A home is assessed at $70,000. The owners have qualified for homestead tax exemption. Assuming a homestead tax exemption of $25,000, what is the taxable value of this home?

Assessed Value − Homestead Exemption = Taxable Value

$70,000   − $25,000   = $45,000

The taxable value is the amount to which the appropriate "tax rate" is applied to determine the amount of property taxes to be paid.

HOW THE PROPERTY TAX RATE IS ESTABLISHED

The following simple formula is used for determining the tax rate of school boards, cities and counties:

$$\text{Tax Rate} = \frac{\text{Estimated Expenses (Budget)} - \text{Non-Property Tax Revenues}}{\text{Total Assessed Valuation} - \text{Exemptions}}$$

$$TR = \frac{EE - NR}{TAV - E}$$

Example: Assume that the county officials of Foamcrest County have approved a budget for next year indicating expected expenditures of $12,500,000. Experience indicates a reasonable expectation of $2,500,000 in revenue from sources other than property taxes. The county property appraiser reports a total assessed valuation of all taxable properties in the amount of $1,075,000,000. Homestead tax exemptions of $25,000 have been granted to each of 3,000 property owners. Apply these figures to the formula to determine the tax rate in the county.

$$\text{Tax Rate} = \frac{\$12,500,000 - \$2,500,000}{\$1,075,000,000 - \$75,000,000}$$

$$= \frac{\$10,000,000}{\$1,000,000,000}$$

$$= .010$$

The tax rate to be applied to all real property in Foamcrest County is .010 of assessed value. This tax rate is usually expressed in mills rather than in decimal form. A *mill* is one thousandth of a dollar. It follows that there are 1,000 mills in a dollar. Thus, the above tax rate of .010 can be expressed as 10 mills per dollar.

To convert the tax rate from a decimal to mills, simply move the decimal point 3 places to the right. Add zeros, if necessary. This is the same as multiplying the decimal by 1,000.

To convert millage to the decimal form, place the decimal point 3 places to the left of the written or unwritten decimal point (for example, 9 mills = .009; 26.8 mills = .0268). This is the same as dividing the mills by 1,000.

When expressing mills in decimal form, always use three digits to avoid possible confusion (for example, 20 mills in decimal form is .020).

Actually, tax rates may be expressed in many ways. For instance, the tax rate of .021 may also be expressed as:

    21 mills per $1 of assessed valuation
    $.021 per $1 of assessed valuation
    $2.10 per $100 of assessed valuation
    $21 per $1,000 of assessed valuation

Practice: The Palmsburg County government has estimated its budget for the coming year to be $24,000,000. Income from nonproperty tax revenues is expected to be $8,000,000. The county property appraiser reports $1,050,000,000 in taxable properties. Exactly 2,000 parcels are eligible for the $25,000 homestead tax exemption. What is the tax rate?

_____ 5-1

APPLYING THE TAX RATE

Using the previously described situation in which a home was assessed at $70,000 and the homeowners qualifed for a homestead tax exemption of $25,000, the calculation of the county property taxes on that home is as follows:

Assessed value	$70,000
Homestead exemption	− 25,000
Taxable value	$45,000
County tax rate	× .016
Annual county property taxes	$720.000 = $720

The tax rate is always applied to the taxable value. Where no exemptions apply, the taxable value and the assessed value are the same. However, if any exemptions do apply, they must be deducted from the assessed value. The result is taxable value. To find the dollar amount of property taxes, always multiply the taxable value by the tax rate:

Assessed Value − Tax Exemption(s) = Taxable Value
Taxable Value × Tax Rate = Dollar Amount of Taxes

Example: Mr. Pasco owns a home in the city. The city tax rate is 8.7 mills, the county tax rate is 9.2 mills, and the school board tax rate is 8 mills. Mr. Pasco has qualified for a homestead tax exemption of $25,000. His home has been assessed at $64,500. What must Mr. Pasco pay in property taxes?

Assessed value	$64,500
Exemption	− 25,000
Taxable value	$39,500
Tax rate (8.7 + 9.2 + 8)	× .0259 (25.9 mills)
Total property taxes	$1,023.0500 = $1,023.05

If Mr. Pasco is interested in finding the amount of savings in property taxes realized by the exemption:

Exemption × Tax Rate = Savings
$25,000   ×   .0259   = $647.50

But what if Mr. Pasco lived outside the city limits in the same county? How much difference, if any, would there be in his property taxes? The solution is exactly the same as above with one exception: subtract the city tax rate of 8.7 mills from the former total of 25.9 mills, leaving a new effective tax rate of 17.2 mills (.0172):

Assessed value	$64,500
Exemption	− 25,000
Taxable value	$39,500
Tax rate (9.2 + 8)	× .0172 (17.2 mills)
Total property taxes	$679.4000 = $679.40

So the difference is $343.65 ($1,023.05 − $679.40 *or* $39,500 × 8.7 mills).

When solving real estate property tax problems, use the memory device once again.

Taxes

$$- \div \ \overline{\top} \ \div -$$

Taxable value = Base
Tax rate = Rate
Amount of taxes = Result

Taxable $\times$ Tax
Value $\quad$ Rate

Example: Find the tax rate if Mr. Pasco paid $980.52 last year in property taxes on property assessed at $86,500. Assume that Mr. Pasco is still qualified for the $25,000 homestead tax exemption.

$980.52

$$- \div \ \overline{\top} \ \div -$$

Taxable value = $86,500 − $25,000
= $61,500

$61,500 $\times$?

Tax rate = $980.52 ÷ $61,500
= .01594 or 15.94 mills

In those states where the assessed value of a property is a percentage of the market value, the memory aid will help establish the assessed value. Use market value as the Base, and use the percent of market value that represents the assessed value for the Rate.

Assessed Value

$$- \div \ \overline{\top} \ \div -$$

Market value = Base
Percent of market value = Rate
Assessed value = Result

Market $\times$ Percent of
Value $\quad$ Market
$\quad$ Value

Example: Assume that the assessed value of a house is 80% of full market value. If the market value is $92,000, what is the assessed value?

?

$$- \div \ \overline{\top} \ \div -$$

Assessed value = $92,000 × 80%
= $92,000 × .80
= $73,600

$92,000 $\times$ 80%

SPECIAL ASSESSMENTS

At this point, notice should be taken of a one-time tax levied on property owners to help pay for some improvement that, in theory at least, adds to the value of their property. The name given to this type of one-time tax is "special assessment."

Example: Suppose you live on an unpaved street. The city is petitioned to pave the street and agrees to do so. The paving cost is found to be $24 per running foot, and the city is to pay 30% of the cost. If your lot frontage on the street is 100 feet, what will your special assessment be for street paving? (Do not forget that the street has two sides, and the property across the street must bear its fair share.)

Lot frontage	=	100 feet
Cost per front foot	=	× $24
Cost to pave 100 feet	=	$2,400
Owners' share of cost (100% − 30%)	=	× .70
Cost to property owners	=	$1,680.00
Your half of street paving cost	=	$840

Practice: The town is assessing all property owners, on the streets affected, for the cost of paving the streets. Property owners will have to pay 65% of the $25-per-running-foot cost. What will the special paving assessment be for a parcel of land with a frontage of 90 feet?

_____ 5-2

REAL PROPERTY TRANSFER TAXES

Most states tax the transfer of real estate. However, the tax rates and the exemptions from taxation vary from state to state. In one state, for example, the tax is $.50 for each $500 of "new money" (new loan) involved, while in another state, a related tax is $.55 for each $100 of the entire purchase price. But the procedures employed for solving problems related to transfer taxes are generally the same, whether the taxes are called revenue stamp taxes, transfer taxes or documentary stamp taxes.

The following is an example of a type of real estate transfer tax that may be levied on real property transfers:

> A state documentary stamp tax on deeds. For instance, this may be assessed at the rate of $.55 for each $100, or any fraction of $100, on the entire purchase price. No exemptions are allowed.

> (Note: The word "documentary" need not cause concern—think about the intent: to imprint or place tax stamps on "documents," such as deeds.)

Example: A farm sold for $115,500. The buyer paid an earnest money deposit of $15,000 and assumed an existing mortgage of $75,000. The seller took back a second mortgage from the buyer for the balance of the purchase price. Using the above-cited rate, how much will the seller need to pay for the state transfer tax?

> State doc. stamp tax on deed:

> $115,500 ÷ $100 = 1,155 taxable increments
> 1,155 × $.55 = $635.25 documentary stamp tax on deed

Example: A house sold for $86,000. The buyer paid $10,000 down and agreed to pay the balance in cash at closing. Using the above-cited rate, how much will the seller pay for the state transfer tax?

> State doc. stamp tax on deed:

> $86,000 ÷ $100 = 860 taxable increments
> 860 × $.55 = $473 doc. stamp tax on deed

As shown in these two examples, this tax on deeds is based on the entire purchase price of a property. How this purchase price is met by the buyer (cash, assumption of mortgage or new mortgage) is not a consideration in this calculation.

The law in most states requires payment of a full increment of tax for any fractional portion of a tax increment. Therefore, any fractional part must be rounded *up* to the next whole taxable increment.

To illustrate, what would have been the cost of the state tax on the deed if the sale price of $115,500 in the first example had been $115,525 instead?

> $115,525 ÷ $100 = 1,155.25 taxable increments
> 1,155.25 rounds up to 1,156 increments
> 1,156 × $.55 = $635.80 ($.55, or one increment more than the example)

What would have been the cost of the state tax on the deed if the sale price of $115,500 had been $115,450 instead?

> $115,450 ÷ $100 = 1,154.5 taxable increments
> 1,154.5 rounds up to 1,155 increments
> 1,155 × $.55 = $635.25 (no change)

This type of situation is encountered so often in the real estate business that further practice is appropriate. It is also useful to practice with problems that include the need to calculate the two state taxes from the previous chapter. Use the following tax rates for the next four problems:

Intangible tax on mortgage: $.002 per dollar of face value
Documentary tax on note: $.32 per $100, or fraction of $100
Documentary tax on deed: $.55 per $100, or fraction of $100

Practice:	Sale price	$72,800	
	FHA mortgage assumed	$59,780	
#1	New second mortgage taken back by seller	$12,020	
	Cash from buyer	$ 1,000	
	State documentary stamp tax on deed	_____	5-3

#2	Sale price	$66,950	
	Buyer paid all cash		
	Documentary stamp tax on deed	_____	5-4

Are there any additional new taxes created by either of the two practice problems above? How about the new second mortgage in practice problem #1? Taxes on new mortgages were explained and practiced in the previous chapter. Now compute all of the state taxes created by the practice problems below:

	#3	Sale price	$73,000	
		Existing mortgage assumed	$57,825	
		Second mortgage to seller	$10,100	
		Cash paid by buyer	$ 5,075	
		Documentary stamps on deed	_____	5-5
		Documentary stamps on note	_____	5-6
		Intangible tax on mortgage	_____	5-7

	#4	Sale price	$89,750	
		Existing mortgage (paid off from proceeds of a new mortgage)	$18,900	
		New mortgage by buyer	$71,800	
		Cash paid by buyer	$17,950	
		Documentary stamps on deed	_____	5-8
		Documentary stamps on note	_____	5-9
		Intangible tax on mortgage	_____	5-10

Because taxes will be involved in every real estate transaction, it is especially important to become proficient at calculating the various relevant taxes. As a further aid, the chapter on closing statements includes the step-by-step procedure for prorating taxes between the buyer and the seller.

REVIEW PROBLEMS

1. Complete the formula below by using abbreviations:

    Tax Rate =

2. The total assessed valuation of real property in the town of Heartman is $440,000,000. The town estimates its next year's budget expenditures to be $11,000,000 and expects $3,800,000 from nonproperty tax revenues. Property belonging to governmental and other totally tax-exempt owners amounts to $2,180,000. In addition, 200 properties have each been granted a $25,000 homestead exemption. What will the tax rate be in mills? (Round to the nearest tenth of a mill.)

    _____

3. In Apple County, next year's estimated expenses will be $10,997,500 with $1,895,000 expected from nonproperty tax revenues. The total taxable assessed valuation is $212,650,000. Exactly 230 properties have qualified for a $25,000 homestead exemption each and 50 properties have been granted a widow's exemption of $500 each. What is the tax rate in mills? (Round to the nearest whole mill.)

    _____

4. The city has agreed to pay 22% of the cost for installing sewer lines in a new subdivision. What will each property owner be required to pay as a special assessment if lots are a standard 100 front feet and the cost of installation is $34 per front foot?

    _____

Calculate the state transfer taxes required on the following two transactions by using the tax rates below:

Documentary stamp tax on deed: $.55 per $100, or fraction of $100
Documentary stamp tax on note: $.32 per $100, or fraction of $100
Intangible tax on mortgage: $.002 per dollar of face value

5. Purchase price $82,400
   Existing VA mortgage (assumed by buyer) $44,000
   New second mortgage $26,400
   Cash from buyer $12,000

   a. Documentary stamps on deed   ———

   b. Documentary stamps on note   ———

   c. Intangible tax on mortgage   ———

6. Purchase price $71,500
   Existing mortgage (paid off by new
       mortgage obtained by buyer) $41,000
   New mortgage to refinance $59,725
   Cash from buyer $11,775

   a. Documentary stamps on deed   ———

   b. Documentary stamps on note   ———

   c. Intangible tax on mortgage   ———

7. Convert mills to decimal numbers.

   a.   1 mill =   _____

   b. 10 mills =   _____

   c. 100 mills =   _____

8. Convert decimal numbers to mills

   a. .016589 =   _____

   b. .003014 =   _____

   c. .03554 =   _____

For the next two problems, calculate the real property taxes due.

9. Assessed value of property $93,700
    Tax rate   26.8 mills
    Exemptions granted   0
    Property taxes due   _____

10. Assessed value of property $74,000
    Tax rate   27.3 mills
    Exemptions granted:
      Homestead $25,000
      Disabled veteran $500
      Widow $500
    Property taxes due   _____

11. In Murray County, real property is assessed at 60% of market value. If a house sells for $76,000 and the tax rate is 16 mills, what are the required property taxes, disregarding exemptions?

_____

• Practice with the memory device (questions 12 through 14).

12. Last year, Mr. Citrus paid $1,054 in property taxes on property with a total taxable value of $59,030. What was the tax rate in mills? (Round to nearest tenth of a mill.)

_____

13. Cascade County used a tax rate of 28 mills to collect $1,736 from Mr. and Mrs. Pine. What was the taxable value of the Pine property?

_____

14. The tax rate in River City is 26.5 mills. What would the property taxes be on a property with a taxable value of $54,000?

_____

Chapter 6

Legal Descriptions and Area Problems

KEY MEASUREMENTS

Linear Measure:

12 inches (12″)	= 1 foot (1 ft.)
3 feet (3′)	= 1 yard (1 yd.)
5,280 feet (5,280′)	= 1 mile (1 mi.) = 1,760 yards

Surface Area Measure:

12 inches × 12 inches	= 144 square inches (144 sq. in.)
1 foot × 1 foot	= 1 square foot (1 sq. ft.)
1 square foot	= 144 square inches
3 feet × 3 feet	= 9 square feet
9 square feet	= 1 square yard (1 sq. yd.)
43,560 square feet	= 1 acre (1 A.)
1 acre	= approximately 208.71′ × 208.71′
1 mile × 1 mile	= 1 square mile
640 acres	= 1 section
1 square mile	= 1 section = 640 acres
36 sections (6 mi. × 6 mi.)	= 1 township (1 T, or 1 TWP)
36 square miles (6 miles square)	= 1 township

Cubic Area (Volume):

12″ × 12″ × 12″ (1 cu. ft.)	= 1,728 cubic inches
3′ × 3′ × 3′ (1 cu. yd.)	= 27 cubic feet
1 board foot	= 144 cubic inches (12″ × 12″ × 1″)
1 cubic foot	= approximately 7.5 gallons

Circular Measure:

60 seconds (60″)	= 1 minute (1′)
60 minutes (60′)	= 1 degree (1°)
90 degrees (90°) in a quadrant	
360 degrees (360°) in a circle	

Metric Equivalents for Linear Measures:

Metric to U.S.		U.S. to Metric	
1 centimeter (1 cm)	= 0.3937 inch	1 inch = 2.54 centimeters	
1 meter (1 m)	= 39.37 inches		
1 meter	= 1.0936 yards	1 yard = 0.9144 meter	
1 kilometer (1 km)	= 0.621 mile	1 mile = 1.609 kilometers	

Four different types of legal descriptions may be encountered in working with real property:

1. Metes and bounds
2. Government land survey
3. Lot and block numbers
4. Monuments

Only the first three methods are recommended because the fourth lacks accuracy. Only the first two will be examined in this book because there is little math associated with the third method.

DESCRIPTION BY METES AND BOUNDS

All real estate professionals should be capable of reading and interpreting a properly written description of land. This ability allows a tract's size and shape to be closely approximated. From this information, the area of a tract can be calculated.

In plotting metes (measurements) and bounds (direction) legal descriptions, the point of beginning (POB) and all turning points should be regarded as the exact center of a circle. Always mentally place the POB at the center of a circle and proceed out in a designated direction.

Every compass and every circle has four cardinal directions:

North
South
East
West

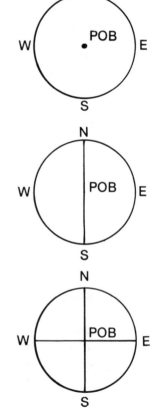

If you draw a straight line connecting North and South, you have identified and connected the two primary direction indicators for plotting metes and bounds legal descriptions. The first movement from the center of a circle will always be outward in either a North or a South direction.

To identify the two secondary direction indicators, draw a straight line connecting East and West. The result is a circle divided into 4 quarters, or quadrants. Because a circle has 360 degrees, each quadrant has a total of 90 degrees.

In metes and bounds legal descriptions, all directions begin with a reference to either North or South—the primary indicators.

Example:

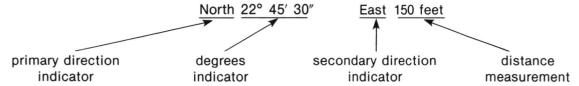

The above direction indicators specify:

1. Proceed from the point of beginning at the center of an imaginary circle North to the edge of the imaginary circle.

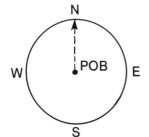

2. At the edge of the circle, proceed in the direction of the secondary direction indicator (East) the number of degrees stated—22° 45′ 30″. Place a mark on the edge of the circle at the approximate place of the specified degree location.

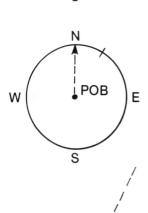

3. Draw a straight line from the center of the circle (POB) extending through the degree location and beyond. This will indicate the tract boundary direction (but not the distance).

N 22° 45′ 30″ E 150′

4. Use a simple scale to indicate the distance (150 feet) the boundary should be extended (1 inch might be used to indicate 100 feet).

Example: From the brass marker at the center of the intersection of Keyes Avenue and Century Street, proceed North 45° 10' 30" West 39.80' to the point of beginning. From POB proceed South 89° 30' 00" West 208.71', thence North 0° 30' 00" West 208.71', thence North 89° 30' 00" East 208.71', thence directly to POB.

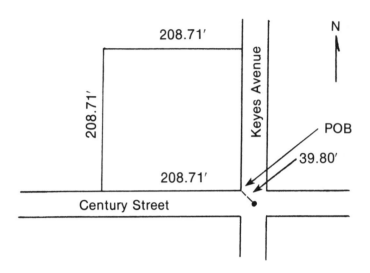

Practice: On the township sketch below, draw the boundary lines of the following metes and bounds legal description:

A tract of land located in Township 14 South, Range 6 East, described as follows:

T14S, R6E

6	5	4	3	2	1
7	8	9	10	11	12
18	17	16	15	14	13
19	20	21	22	23	24
30	29	28	27	26	25
31	32	33	34	35	36

Beginning at a point of beginning located on the Southeast corner of Section 4, proceed South 45° East to the Northwest corner of Section 24, thence proceed South 45° West to the Northeast corner of Section 33, thence North 45° West to the Southeast corner of Section 18, thence North 45° East to the POB.

6-1

GOVERNMENT LAND SURVEY SYSTEM

The government land survey system, also called the rectangular survey method, is a system of numbered squares, as shown below. The primary units of measurement in this system are:

Township: a square, 6 miles on each side (36 square miles), divided into 36 sections.

Section: a square, 1 mile on each side (1 square mile). The 36 sections in each township are all numbered and identified in the sequence below.

Township 1 South, Range 1 West

36	31					36	31
1	6	5	4	3	2	1	6
	7	8	9	10	11	12	
	18	17	16	15	14	13	
	19	20	21	22	23	24	
	30	29	28	27	26	25	
36	31	32	33	34	35	36	31
1	6					1	6

N

Each section contains 640 acres and is commonly subdivided into halves, quarters and smaller tracts.

To subdivide a section:

    1. Through the center of a section, draw a vertical line from top to bottom (North to South).

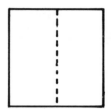

    2. Again through the center, draw a horizontal line (West to East).

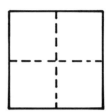

    3. The section is now divided into 4 quarters. The upper right corner of the section is the Northeast Quarter, the lower right corner is the Southeast Quarter, etc., as shown.

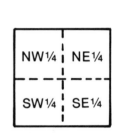

Each quarter section contains 160 acres. To locate a smaller tract, subdivide a quarter section by drawing vertical and/or horizontal lines until you have reduced the area to the size of the desired tract.

To locate property from a legal description, always begin at the *end* of the description and work back from right to left.

Example: Locate the Southeast ¼ of the Northwest ¼ of Section 24.

    First, locate Section 24, then locate the Northwest ¼ of Section 24.
Then, subdivide the quarter section into 4 quarters and locate the Southeast ¼ of that subdivision.

Section 24

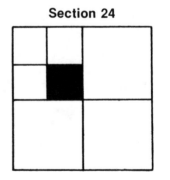

Example: Locate the N½ of the NE¼ of the SE¼ of Section 12.
                        (3)   (2)   (1)

(1) Locate the SE¼.

(2) Locate the NE¼ of the SE¼.

(3) Locate the N½ of the NE¼ of the SE¼.

Section 12

Practice: Locate the NE¼ of the SE¼ of the NW¼ of
Section 36.

Section 36

6-2

Calculating Number of Acres

To determine the number of acres in a tract that is properly described, simple arithmetic is used. Multiply the denominator of each fraction by its neighboring denominator, one after the next, until all have been multiplied. Then divide the result into 640 acres (1 section = 640 acres) to learn the number of acres in the tract described.

Example: Using the Practice description above, find the number of acres:

NE¼, SE¼, NW¼ of Section 36

Denominators: 4 × 4 × 4 = 64

640 acres ÷ 64 = 10 acres in the tract

This process is actually an abbreviated method of multiplying 640 acres by the fractions (numerators will always be 1) in the legal description:

$$\frac{1}{4} \times \frac{1}{4} \times \frac{1}{4} \times 640 \text{ acres} = \frac{640}{64} = 10 \text{ acres}$$

Practice: How many acres are contained in a tract described as:

SW$\frac{1}{4}$ of the NE$\frac{1}{4}$ of Section 3   _____ 6-3

The following is another method of finding the number of acres in a parcel and also follows the pattern of locating tracts by starting at the end of the legal description and working backward. The two methods provide alternate ways to check for accuracy.

Alternate Method. This method is also based on the fact that every section has 640 acres. To find the number of acres in a description:

(a) Divide 640 acres by the last denominator in the description.

(b) Divide the answer from (a) by the next to last denominator.

(c) Continue to the left, each time dividing the last answer by the next denominator.

Example: N½   SW¼   SE¼   Section 6

The answer is 20 acres.

Example: E½   NW¼   SE¼   NE¼   Section 21

5 ◄————— 10 ◄——— 40 ◄——— 160 ◄——— 640 acres

The answer is 5 acres.

Practice: W$\frac{1}{2}$ E$\frac{1}{2}$ NW$\frac{1}{4}$ Section 2

_____ 6-4

When a legal description contains the word "and," calculate the number of acres and stop on reaching "and." Begin a new calculation on the other side of the "and." Now add the two acreages.

Example: How many acres are contained in a tract described as the S½, SW¼, SE¼ Section 6 and the N½, NW¼, NE¼ Section 7?

Section 7 = 4 × 4 × 2 = 32   640 ÷ 32 = 20 acres
Section 6 = 4 × 4 × 2 = 32   640 ÷ 32 = 20 acres
                 Total acres in tract: 40 acres

Converting Square Feet to Acres. To find the exact number of acres in a parcel when square feet are involved, divide the number of square feet by 43,560 square feet per acre. This is the most commonly used method for converting square feet to acres.

But because more mistakes seem to be made when dividing than when multiplying, the *factor-of-23 method* may be helpful. This method uses "23" because one square foot is approximately .000023 of an acre (1 sq. ft. ÷ 43,560 sq. ft. = approximately .000023). This procedure avoids dividing entirely and is accurate to 1/100 of one acre. However, as the number of acres increases, the accuracy decreases.

Steps to take to use the factor-of-23 method:

1. Determine the number of square feet involved.

2. Multiply the total number of square feet by 23.

3. Place a decimal point 6 places to the left of the last digit in the answer.

In the following example, the two methods are shown. Compare their accuracy.

Example: Calculate the number of acres in a tract that measures 460′ × 490′.

$$460′ × 490′ = 225,400 \text{ sq. ft.}$$

225,400 sq. ft. ÷ 43,560 sq. ft./acre

= 5.1744719 acres

= 5.2 acres (rounded)

225,400 sq. ft. × 23 acres
= 5184200
= 5 184200.
= 5.2 acres (rounded)

For each practice problem involving the conversion of square feet to acres, first use the "43,560 method" to obtain the exact answer and then the factor-of-23 method for comparison. (For all examples hereafter, the more accurate 43,560 sq. ft./acre method is used.)

Practice: How many acres are there in 44,500 square feet?

_____ 6-5

How many acres are there in 140,400 square feet?

_____ 6-6

Practice: Write the legal description and then determine the number of acres in each of the 8 lettered areas of Section 4 below:

	Legal Description	Number of Acres	

Section 4

a. _____ _____ 6-7

b. _____ _____ 6-8

c. _____ _____ 6-9

d. _____ _____ 6-10

e. _____ _____ 6-11

f. _____ _____ 6-12

g. _____ _____ 6-13

h. _____ _____ 6-14

i. Mr. Duval wants to buy a parcel measuring 1,935' by 1,800'. If neighboring land has recently sold for $800 per acre, how much should Mr. Duval expect to pay? (Round the number of acres to the nearest whole acre.)

_____ 6-15

j. Mr. Walton owned the SW¼ of a section. He sold the East ½ of that Southwest Quarter. How many acres does Mr. Walton still own?

_____ 6-16

k. The city aviation authority bought a tract of farmland described as the S½ of the N½ of the SE¼ of Section 8. A total of $640,000 was paid for the land. What was the cost per acre?

_____ 6-17

SOLVING UNKNOWN AREA PROBLEMS

Key Math Terms

Angle:

Acute angle: where two intersecting lines meet to form an angle of less than 90 degrees (0 to 90 degrees). (Think of "cute" as small.)

Obtuse angle: where two intersecting lines meet to form an angle that is greater than 90 degrees (90^+ to 180 degrees). (Think of "obtuse" as obese.)

Right angle: where two intersecting lines meet exactly perpendicular to each other (90 degrees).

Area: the amount of surface contained within a described boundary. Stated in square units, such as square feet.

Base: that side of a geometric figure on which the figure should rest.

Circle: a closed curved line on which every point is equidistant from the center.

Circumference: the circular distance around the boundary of a circle.

Diameter: the straight line distance across a circle through the center.

Height: the perpendicular distance from the base of a geometric figure to the highest point.

Perimeter: the lines forming the outside boundaries of a figure. Perimeter equals the sum of all the sides.

Pi (π):   a mathematical factor used to determine the circumference of a circle. For real estate purposes, use $\pi = 3.1416$.

Radius: the straight line distance from the center of a circle to the edge (one-half the diameter).

Volume: the amount of space within a confined three-dimensional object (cubic measure).

To determine the area of any tract, the general shape must be known (square, triangle, and so forth). When a legal description is involved, it must be read carefully. Then, sketch the boundaries described as near to scale as possible to reveal the shape of the tract. Then use the correct formula for the shape involved.

Parallelogram: a four-sided plane figure whose opposite sides are parallel and equal in length; includes squares and rectangles but is ordinarily used to refer to a figure with two acute angles and two obtuse angles.

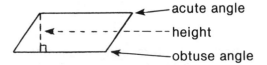

Rectangle: a four-sided figure whose opposite sides are parallel and equal in length and whose angles are all right angles (a parallelogram with four right angles).

Square: a four-sided figure bounded by four lines of equal length whose angles are all right angles (a parallelogram with four equal sides and four right angles).

Triangle: a three-sided figure with three angles.

a. Equilateral triangle: a triangle whose sides are equal in length.

b. Isosceles triangle: a triangle with two sides equal in length.

c. Right-angle triangle: a triangle with a right angle.

d. Scalene triangle: a triangle with three unequal sides.

Trapezoid: a four-sided figure with only two sides parallel and four angles, which may be right angles, acute angles, or obtuse angles.

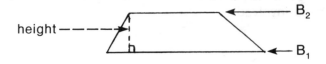

Formulas to Use in Unknown Area Problems

1. For all *squares, rectangles,* and *parallelograms,* use the following formula:

    Area = Base × Height

    A = B × H

2. For all *triangles,* use the following formula:

    Area = Base × Height ÷ 2

    $$A = \frac{B \times H}{2} \quad \text{or,} \quad A = \tfrac{1}{2}B \times H$$

3. For all *trapezoids,* use the following formula:

    Area = (Base One + Base Two) ÷ 2 × Height

    $$A = \frac{(B_1 + B_2)}{2} \times H \quad \text{or,} \quad A = \tfrac{1}{2}(B_1 + B_2) \times H$$

    Of the two parallel sides, either one may be used as B_1 or B_2.

4. For all *circles*, use the following formulas:

    a. To find the *area* of a circle:

    Area = Pi × Radius squared

    $$A = \pi \times r^2 \quad \text{or simply,} \quad A = \pi r^2$$

    To "square" a number means to multiply it by itself.

    b. To find the *circumference* of a circle:

    Circumference = Pi × Diameter

    $$C = \pi \times d \quad \text{or simply,} \quad C = \pi d$$

    Circumference = 2 × Pi × Radius

    $$C = 2 \times \pi \times r \quad \text{or simply,} \quad C = 2\pi r$$

Formulas to Use in Cubic Measure (Volume) Problems

From time to time, it is necessary to determine the volume of a room, building or other enclosure, such as a silo. Volume is always expressed in cubic units (cubic inches, and so forth).

To calculate volume, one step of computation is added to the calculation of area. It involves a third dimension in addition to the dimensions required to find area.

1. To find the volume (cubic measure) of all *squares* and *rectangles*, use the following formula:

$$\text{Volume} = \text{Length} \times \text{Width} \times \text{Height}$$

$$V = L \times W \times H \text{ or simply, } V = LWH$$

2. To find the volume of a *cylinder*, use the following formula:

$$\text{Volume} = \text{Pi} \times \text{Radius squared} \times \text{Height}$$

$$V = \pi \times r^2 \times H \text{ or simply, } V = \pi r^2 H$$

A cylinder should be visualized as a circle with height added. Thus, the above formula is the area of a circle times its height.

Example: The front and back boundaries of a parcel are parallel to each other. Both are 400 feet long. The two sides are also parallel and also 400 feet long. How many acres are contained in the property?

A sketch reveals that the tract must be a square or a parallelogram. The formula used to determine the area for either (as well as the area of a rectangle) is:

$A = B \times H$

$= 400' \times 400'$

$= 160,000 \text{ sq. ft.}$

$= 160,000 \text{ sq. ft.} \div 43,560 \text{ sq. ft./acre}$

$= 3.67 \text{ acres in the parcel}$

Example: The parcel of property located on the corner of Watson Avenue & Conder Street has for a base side 150 feet of frontage on Watson Avenue and a side 100 feet parallel to Conder Street. The third side is 180 feet. How many acres are included in these boundaries?

By sketching the property boundaries at a street intersection, you see that the base side (B) is the boundary line paralleling Watson Avenue. From this point, you sketch in the boundary on Conder Street which turns out to be the height boundary (H). The third boundary merely connects the two previously described boundaries. When you see the shape of the property, you know which formula to apply.

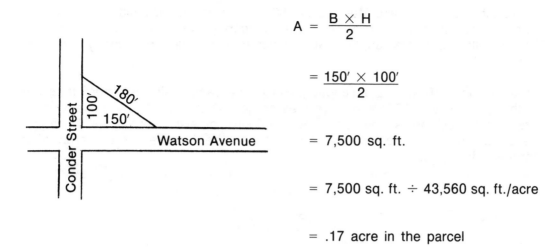

$$A = \frac{B \times H}{2}$$

$$= \frac{150' \times 100'}{2}$$

$$= 7,500 \text{ sq. ft.}$$

$$= 7,500 \text{ sq. ft.} \div 43,560 \text{ sq. ft./acre}$$

$$= .17 \text{ acre in the parcel}$$

While the same procedure and the same formula apply to any three-sided tract of property, remember that the height is the perpendicular distance from the base to the highest point.

Example: A tract of land is 200 feet on its base side. Two other boundary lines are each 166 feet long and extend from the two ends of the base side to a point where they intersect exactly 132 feet from the midpoint of the base side. How many acres are contained within the boundaries?

By sketching the base line first and connecting two lines, one from each end of the base side, you see an isosceles triangle (a triangle with two sides equal in length).

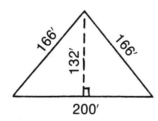

The height (H) must be the perpendicular distance from the base (B) to the highest point. In this case the intersection of the two lines is the highest point. The distance from that point of intersection to the base side is 132 feet, so H is 132 feet and B is 200 feet.

$$A = \frac{B \times H}{2}$$

$$= \frac{200' \times 132'}{2}$$

$$= 13,200 \text{ sq. ft.}$$

$$= 13,200 \text{ sq. ft.} \div 43,560 \text{ sq. ft./acre}$$

$$= .3 \text{ acre in the tract}$$

Example: A residential lot on Lake Maitland is 150 feet on one parallel side and 120 feet on the opposite parallel side. The west boundary of the lot is 110 feet and joins the parallel sides at an angle of 90 degrees on both sides. How many acres are in the lot?

Sketch the lot from the description. Since one parallel side is longer than the other (150′ versus 120′) and since they are joined at one side by a line forming two 90 degree angles, you can produce a figure somewhat as follows. Once you see the shape of the lot, you know to use the formula for the area of a trapezoid:

$$A = \frac{(B_1 + B_2)}{2} \times H$$

$$= \frac{(150' + 120')}{2} \times 110'$$

$$= \frac{270'}{2} \times 110'$$

$$= 14{,}850 \text{ sq. ft.}$$

$$= 14{,}850 \text{ sq. ft.} \div 43{,}560 \text{ sq. ft./acre}$$

$$= .34 \text{ acre in the lot}$$

It is not unusual to find that the shape of a parcel of real property does not conform to that of a square, rectangle, triangle and so forth. When this occurs, it is normally possible to divide the parcel into a series of figures that conform to common shapes.

Example: A parcel is shaped and measures as shown in the diagram. What is the total area of the parcel of land in square feet?

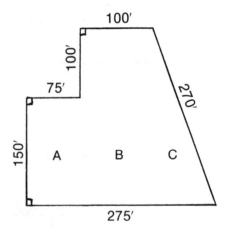

The above parcel can be divided into three common geometric figures: two rectangles and one triangle:

rectangle A: 150' × 75' = 11,250 sq. ft.

rectangle B: 250' × 100' = 25,000 sq. ft.

triangle C: $\dfrac{100' \times 250'}{2}$ = 12,500 sq. ft.

_____

Total area of parcel   = 48,750 sq. ft.

Note: (Perhaps you have discovered that the above parcel could have been divided, instead, into one rectangle (A) and one trapezoid (BC). As is often the case, "explanations, problems and solutions" can be approached in more than one way and still produce the same result. You are encouraged to try different approaches to check your understanding and answers.)

Example: Mrs. Flagler plans to build a fence around a circular flower bed. The straight line distance across the center of her flower bed is 12 feet.

a. How many feet of fencing will be required to encircle the flower bed?

b. What amount of area will be enclosed within the fence?

1. Solve for circumference.

$C = \pi \times d$

$= 3.1416 \times 12'$

$= 37.6992$ or 38 feet of fencing

2. Solve for area.

$A = \pi \times r^2$

$= 3.1416 \times (6')^2$

$= 3.1416 \times 36$ sq. ft.

$= 113.0976$ or 113 square feet enclosed

Example: Mr. Polk built a storage silo with an inside diameter of 14 feet. The interior height was 30 feet. What is the volume of the silo?

$V = \pi \times r^2 \times H$

$= 3.1416 \times (7')^2 \times 30'$

$= 3.1416 \times 49$ sq. ft. $\times 30'$

$= 4,618.152$ cubic feet

Example: Dorothy wants to build a swimming pool 16 feet by 54 feet by 9 feet. How many cubic yards of earth must be excavated to provide the space for the pool?

$$V = L \times W \times H$$
$$= 54' \times 16' \times 9'$$
$$= 7{,}776 \text{ cubic feet}$$
$$= 7{,}776 \text{ cu. ft.} \div 27 \text{ cu. ft./cu. yd.}$$
$$= 288 \text{ cubic yards of earth}$$

Cost Per Unit

Quite often, a real estate practitioner must determine the cost per square foot, or the cost per acre, of a parcel of real property.

Example: If the cost of a 57,575-square-foot residential lot is $23,030, what would the cost per square foot be?

$$\text{Cost} = \text{Sales Price} \div \text{Total Square Footage}$$

$$= \frac{\$23{,}030}{57{,}575 \text{ sq. ft.}}$$

$$= \$.40 \text{ per square foot}$$

The same procedure is utilized to compute the cost per acre.

$$\text{Cost} = \text{Sales Price} \div \text{Number of Acres}$$

$$= \frac{\$23{,}030}{57{,}575 \text{ sq. ft.} \div 43{,}560 \text{ sq. ft./acre}}$$

$$= \frac{\$23{,}030}{1.321740128 \text{ acres}}$$

$$= \$17{,}424 \text{ per acre}$$

Note that acres or square feet are *always* divided into dollars. Most errors occur when the reverse is done.

REVIEW PROBLEMS

1. What is the perimeter distance around a township?   _____

2. How many sections are in a township?   _____

3. How many square feet are in one acre?   _____

4. How many acres are contained in one section?   _____

5. How many acres are in the NE¼ of NW¼ of Section 1?   _____

6. Draw a line in the circle to show the direction of a boundary line running South 45 degrees East.

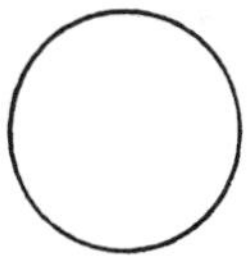

Section X

For questions 7 and 8, draw and blacken the indicated legal descriptions in the blank section and then find the acreage for each:

7. N½, SE¼, SW¼ of Section X: _____

8. NE¼, NE¼, NE¼, SE¼ of Section X: _____

9. How many acres are included in a property described as:
   NW¼ of the SE¼ *and* S½ of the SW¼ of the NE¼ of Section 23?

   _____

10. You have listed for sale a triangular-shaped tract at the intersection of a state highway and an interstate highway. The tract has 1,850 feet of frontage on the interstate and a perpendicular boundary of 3,061 feet frontage on the state highway. The owner wants $15,000 per acre, which includes your sales commission. How many acres (to the nearest whole acre) are in the tract, and what is the sale price?

   _____

   _____

11. A residential lot is located in a subdivision with setback restrictions of 25 feet from the street. If the lot has a frontage of 110 feet on the street and a depth of 125 feet, how many square feet are useless for construction as a result of the setback requirement?

   _____

12. A five-acre tract has a frontage of 330 feet on a road. How deep is the tract?

_____

13. A suite of offices measuring 15 feet by 60 feet rents for $540 per month. What is the cost per square foot per year?

_____

14. How many acres are in a parcel described as follows:

"Beginning at a point on the North side of Highway 101 exactly 200.54 feet West of a cement marker at the intersection of Academy Street and Highway 101; from point of beginning running thence South 90 degrees West 671.2 feet; thence North 0 degrees West 200 feet; thence running North 90 degrees East 200 feet; thence running directly to point of beginning."

_____

15. A developer bought a lot 110 feet wide by 150 feet deep for $6,600. He later bought an adjoining lot 130 feet wide by 150 feet deep for $11,700. He divided the two lots into three equal tracts and sold each of them for $8,540. What percent of profit did he make on the entire transaction?

_____

16. Mr. Rubiosa wants to build a circular swimming pool behind his house. From the center of the proposed pool to the edge is 18 feet. What will the circumference of the pool be? What will the area enclosed inside the circumference be?

_____

_____

17. The village of Oak View built a water processing tank 40 feet high with an inside diameter of 20 feet.

What is the tank's volume?   _____

How many gallons will it hold?   _____
(Refer to Key Measurements, if needed.)

18. A waterfront lot is 150 feet by 200 feet. The owner has offered it for sale at $40,500. What will the cost per square foot be?

_____

19. How many square feet are in the property sketched below?

_____

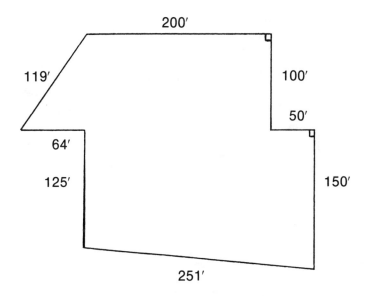

20. A home that is 26 feet by 54 feet has a family room addition underway measuring 16 feet by 28 feet. How many square feet will the enlarged home contain?

_____

Chapter 7

Math In Appraising and Investing

The need to "estimate the value of real property" is a constant and important activity. So is the need to analyze financial and investment matters pertaining to income-producing properties. Real estate appraising and investing are very specialized fields and far too comprehensive to be dealt with here, except to focus on the use of numbers as they apply to estimating property values and analyzing investment properties.

Real property is usually appraised by one or more of the following three methods: the cost, the income or the market comparison approach.

THE COST APPROACH TO ESTIMATING VALUE

The basic factors in the cost (cost-depreciation) approach to estimating value may be expressed in a formula.

Estimated Property Value = Building Reproduction Cost New −
Accrued Depreciation + Land Value

All of the factors in the cost approach are estimates. "Building reproduction cost new" is the amount required to duplicate exactly the building being appraised. "Depreciation" is any loss in value for any reason. "Accrued depreciation" is the total depreciation that has accumulated over the years a building has been standing; it is the difference (loss) in value between an existing building and an exact replica in new condition. Land value is estimated as if the site were vacant. Land is not depreciated.

The total cost to reproduce a building is the basis for all cost approach problems. In appraising, the total cost to reproduce is a combination of two important factors:

Accrued Depreciation + Remaining Building Value =
Total Cost to Reproduce

The knowledge that accrued depreciation plus remaining building value constitute 100% of the cost to reproduce a building is valuable because it means that if any two of the three factors are known, the third can be calculated.

97

Depreciation as an Amount

The simplest way to figure depreciation is the straight-line method. This method spreads the total depreciation over the estimated useful life (economic life) of a building in equal annual amounts.

Depreciation may be found by dividing the dollar cost to reproduce the building new by the total years of useful life:

$$\text{Annual Depreciation} = \text{Total Cost to Reproduce New} \div \text{Years of Useful Life}$$

Example: The cost to reproduce a building new is $116,000. The total years of economic life have been determined to be 40 years. What is the amount of annual depreciation?

$$\text{Annual depreciation} = \$116,000 \div 40 \text{ years}$$
$$= \$2,900$$

To find the amount of accrued depreciation, multiply the annual depreciation by the building's effective age:

$$\text{Accrued Depreciation} = \text{Annual Depreciation} \times \text{Effective Age of the Building}$$

Example: Using the previous problem, what is the loss to accrued depreciation if 8 years is the effective age of the building?

$$\text{Accrued depreciation} = \$2,900 \times 8 \text{ years}$$
$$= \$23,200$$

Assuming the estimated land value of the above property is $20,000, what is the appraised value (estimated value)?

$$\text{Estimated Property Value} = \text{Building Reproduction Cost New} - \text{Accrued Depreciation} + \text{Land Value}$$

$$\text{Estimated property value} = \$116,000 - \$23,200 + \$20,000$$
$$= \$112,800$$

Depreciation as a Percent

Depreciation may also be expressed as a Rate (percent). The total depreciation possible may be expressed as 100%.

To find the depreciation rate per year using the straight-line method, divide 100% (the total depreciation expressed as a percent) by the total years of useful life of the building:

Base   = total years of useful life
Rate   = annual percent of depreciation
Result = total depreciation expressed as 100%

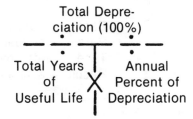

Example: A building has an estimated total useful life of 40 years. What is the annual rate of depreciation?

Base   = 40 years
Rate   = ?
Result = 100%

Annual rate of depreciation =

100% ÷ 40 years = 2.5%

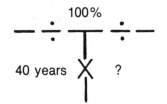

Note: Thus, from the above, the building is said to lose 2.5% of its value per year. This may or may not be true, but calculations are based on this being true.

What would the estimated economic life of the above building have been if it were being depreciated at 2% per year?

Economic life = 100% ÷ 2% per year

= 50 years

The following example shows how to find accrued depreciation as a rate and as an amount once the annual depreciation rate is known.

Example: If the annual depreciation rate is 2.5% and the building has an effective age of 8 years, what is the accrued depreciation expressed as a percent?

Accrued depreciation rate = 2.5% per year × 8 years
                          = 20%

If the cost to reproduce the building new is $116,000, what is the accrued depreciation expressed as an amount?

Accrued depreciation = $116,000 × 20%
                     = $23,200

The variables used in the above example to find accrued depreciation may be expressed in one memory aid:

Base   = cost to reproduce new
Rate   = annual depreciation rate
Time   = effective age
Result = accrued depreciation

Accrued depreciation = $116,000 × 2.5% per year × 8 years
                     = $23,200

Example: The estimated cost to reproduce a house is $75,000. Its current depreciated value has been estimated to be $61,500 with an effective age of 6 years. What is the annual rate of depreciation?

What is missing? Answer: the Rate
What is known?
   Effective age: 6 years
   Total cost to reproduce $75,000
   Current depreciated value   − 61,500
   Accrued depreciation $13,500

Annual rate of depreciation = $13,500 ÷ ($75,000 × 6 years)
                            = $13,500 ÷ $450,000
                            = 3%

Suppose you are asked what the estimated remaining current value of a building is. The amount of accrued depreciation is subtracted from the total cost to reproduce the building new to find the remaining current value of the building.

From the example at the top of the page:

Remaining current value = $116,000 − $23,200
                        = $92,800

Remaining current value (expressed as a percent) may be determined by first subtracting the accrued depreciation rate from the total cost to reproduce the building new expressed as a percent (100%). Then multiply that remaining rate result times the dollar cost to reproduce the building new to find the remaining current value.

Again referring to the above example in which the accrued depreciation rate was 20%:

Remaining rate = 100% − 20%
                       = 80%

As shown in the memory device:

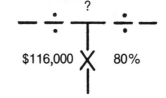

Remaining
Current Value

Cost to ╳ Remaining
Reproduce   Rate

Base   = cost to reproduce
Rate   = remaining rate
Result = remaining current value

?

Remaining current value =
$116,000 × 80% = $92,800

$116,000 ╳ 80%

The memory aid can also help with other common situations.

Example: The remaining current value of a building with an effective age of 5 years is $70,000, independent of land value. Originally, the economic life of the structure was estimated at 50 years. What is the cost to reproduce the building?

What is missing? Answer: the cost to reproduce (Base), the annual depreciation rate (Rate) and the current value expressed as a percent (Rate).

What is known?
Remaining current value $70,000
Economic life   50 years
Effective age of building   5 years
Total depreciation expressed as a percent   100%

By first expressing remaining current value (Result) as a percent of the cost to reproduce (Rate), the cost to reproduce (Base) can then be found.

Find the annual depreciation rate:

Annual depreciation rate =

100% ÷ 50 years = 2%

Accrued depreciation rate =

2% annual depreciation rate × 5 years = 10%

Remaining current value =

100% − 10%   = 90%

Cost to reproduce = $70,000 ÷ 90%
                              = $77,777.78
                              = $77,800 (rounded)

Practice: You are appraising an industrial property for which the land value is estimated to be $80,000. The 15,000-square-foot building is 6 years old and had an economic life when new of 50 years. It would cost $32 per square foot to reproduce the structure today. The site location next to a paper mill has resulted in an external obsolescence depreciation of $19,000. What is the current estimated value of the property?

_____ 7-1

THE INCOME APPROACH TO ESTIMATING VALUE

The second method of evaluating the worth of real property uses a capitalization rate and the net income produced by the property to determine the property value. This approach is sometimes called the income capitalization method or the IRV method.

The basic formula used by appraisers to solve income approach problems in real estate appraising is:

Estimated Property Value = Net Income ÷ Capitalization Rate

$$V = \frac{I}{R}$$

"Net income" is revenue from property or business after expenses have been deducted.

$$\text{Net Income} = \text{Capitalization Rate} \times \text{Property Value}$$
$$\text{I} = \text{RV}$$

For the purposes of this book, regard "capitalization rate" as a percent of return on investment.

$$\text{Capitalization Rate} = \text{Net Income} \div \text{Property Value}$$

$$R = \frac{I}{V}$$

Once again, remember that "appraising" is a complex subject, and the focus here is limited to the math aspects of appraising. Thus, do not be concerned about how to obtain net income and capitalization rate data. Those numbers will be provided for you.

The memory aid is of assistance in solving income approach problems because it incorporates all three of the above formulas:

Base   = property value or total investment
Rate   = capitalization rate
Result = net income or expected
         return on investment

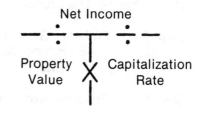

Example: An apartment complex has an annual net income of $22,400. An appraiser has recommended a capitalization rate of 14% for this particular property. What would an investor be justified in paying for the property if the capitalization rate and net income are correct?

Base   = ?
Rate   = 14%
Result   = $22,400
Property value = $22,400 ÷ 14%
                = $160,000 (the amount an investor
                  would be justified in paying)

Practice: The net income from a commercial building is $18,000. The value of the property is $150,000 as estimated by an appraiser. What capitalization rate did the appraiser use to arrive at this value?

_____ 7-2

Net income is used in solving appraising problems via the income approach. However, you may sometimes be given income and expense data and be asked to find the net income of a property. The procedure is as follows:

Step 1   Potential Gross Income −
        Estimated Vacancy and Collection Losses =
        Effective Gross Income

Step 2   Effective Gross Income −
        Operating Expenses =
        Net Income

Example: An apartment complex has 10 three-bedroom units renting for $525 per month and 40 two-bedroom units renting for $450 per month. Vacancy and collection losses in that area are averaging approximately 5%. If the following expenses apply and a capitalization rate of 12.75% is used, what is the appraised value of the apartment complex?

Annual expenses:	Taxes	$37,500
	Insurance	$ 3,050
	Maintenance	$24,000
	Management fee	$25,400
	Utilities	$36,000
	Trash and garbage	$ 4,100
	Reserve for replacements	$33,000

The net income (Result) must be found before the appraised value (Base) can be found. To find the net income, follow steps 1 and 2 above. The potential gross income is found as if every apartment were rented 100% of the time and a deduction is made for expected vacancies. Estimated vacancy and collection losses is a percent of this potential gross income (5% in this example).

Income:

10 apts. @ $525/mo. × 12 months	$ 63,000	
40 apts. @ $450/mo. × 12 months	216,000	
Potential gross income	$279,000	
Estimated vacancy and collection losses (5% × $279,000)	13,950	
Effective gross income		$265,050

Operating Expenses:
    Fixed Expenses:

Taxes	$37,500	
Insurance	3,050	
	$40,550	

    Variable Expenses:

Maintenance	$24,000	
Management fee	25,400	
Utilities	36,000	
Trash and garbage	4,100	
	$89,500	

Reserve for replacements	$33,000	
Total Expenses		$163,050
Net income:		$102,000

Base   = appraised value = ?

Rate   = capitalization rate = 12.75%

Result = net income = $102,000

$102,000 ÷ 12.75% = $800,000

This figure, $800,000, is the appraised value via the income approach.

Practice: What is the appraised value of the following property?

Potential gross income $72,000

Vacancy and collection losses (6%)

Operating Expenses:

Management	$ 6,000
Maintenance	$ 1,280
Utilities	$ 7,600
Taxes	$ 9,020
Insurance	$ 1,100
Reserve for replacements	$13,680
Trash removal	$ 1,000

Capitalization rate   12.5%   _____   7-3

THE MARKET COMPARISON APPROACH TO ESTIMATING VALUE

The third approach involves an evaluation of real property by comparing it to similar properties that have sold recently (comparable sales). This approach to estimating value is also called the market approach and the comparable sales approach. Real estate appraisers may use physical characteristics or income-production characteristics or a combination of both for comparison purposes.

Physical Comparison of Comparable Properties

The value of vacant lots is often estimated by reviewing the prices paid for similar neighboring lots. A common unit of comparison, such as cost per square foot or front foot, is used to equalize variations in value due to size and shape.

Example: What is the estimated market value of a subject lot that is 110 feet by 120 feet?

Recent comparable sales:
Sale 1. A lot 100′ × 120′ located across the street from subject property, sold for $6,800.
Sale 2. A lot 110′ × 120′ in the same neighborhood as subject lot, sold for $7,000.
Sale 3. A lot 100′ × 100′ in a separate but similar quality neighborhood, sold for $6,000.
Sale 4. A lot 130′ × 150′ located in a similar neighborhood, sold for $9,800.

	Price	Size		Price Per Sq. Ft.
Sale 1.	$6,800 ÷	12,000 sq. ft. =	$	.5667 per sq. ft.
Sale 2.	$7,000 ÷	13,200 sq. ft. =		.5303 per sq. ft.
Sale 3.	$6,000 ÷	10,000 sq. ft. =		.6000 per sq. ft.
Sale 4.	$9,800 ÷	19,500 sq. ft. =		.5026 per sq. ft.
				$2.1996

Average price per sq. ft. = $2.1996 ÷ 4 sales
= $ .5499
= $ .55 (rounded)

(Assumes all lots are identical in desirability)

Square footage of subject lot (110′ × 120′) = 13,200 sq. ft.
Average price per square foot (comparables) = ×   .55
Estimated market value of subject lot   = $7,260

Practice: What is the estimated market value of a subject lot measuring 90′ × 120′ if the following five comparables are of equal desirability?

Sale 1. Adjoins subject lot, measures 100′ × 110′, sold for $7,700.
Sale 2. Across the street from subject lot, is 90′ × 110′, sold for $6,850.
Sale 3. A lot 110′ × 110′ on same street in the next block, sold for $8,590.
Sale 4. A lot two lots removed, measures 100′ × 120′, sold for $8,760.
Sale 5. A lot in the next subdivision of similar quality, is 100′ × 120′, sold for $8,650.

Estimated market value of subject lot: _____ 7-4

Gross Rent Multiplier and Gross Income Multiplier

The gross rent multiplier (GRM) and the gross income multiplier (GIM) are alternate means of estimating real property value by the income a property produces. For small residential properties, the gross monthly rental is commonly used, and the ratio derived is called the "gross rent multiplier." For larger residential and for commercial and industrial properties, the gross annual income is used, and the resulting ratio is termed the "gross income multiplier." Both convert income produced into a market value. Both are local in nature and must be determined for each local area at the time a transaction is being considered.

To calculate either a gross rent multiplier or a gross income multiplier, information is collected from sales of similar properties. A relationship is then developed for each property by dividing each sale price by its monthly or annual gross rent.

Gross Rent Multiplier = Sale price ÷ Monthly Gross Income
Gross Income Multiplier = Sale price ÷ Annual Gross Income

Example: The following is an illustration of the calculation of a monthly gross rent multiplier:

Sale Number	Sale Price	Monthly Rental	Monthly Gross Rent Multiplier
1	$89,100	$710	125.49
2	$84,420	$650	129.88
3	$90,785	$740	122.68
4	$87,750	$700	125.36
5	$92,480	$750	123.31
			Average = 125.34

An appraiser would probably use 125 as a monthly gross rent multiplier as a result of the above market analysis. The multiplier is then multiplied by the actual or expected monthly rental income from the property being appraised.

Example: Assume that you are appraising a property that produces a monthly income of $675. Apply the monthly gross rent multiplier above to find the appraised value.

Appraised value = $675 monthly rental × 125 monthly GRM
= $84,375

Practice: Calculate the market value of a fully occupied office building that is producing $210,000 annual gross income (round average multiplier to nearest tenth). Comparable property sales and income data reveal:

Sale Number	Sale Price	Annual Rental	Annual Gross Income Multiplier
1	$1,900,000	$216,000	_____
2	$1,575,000	$187,500	_____
3	$2,200,000	$256,700	_____
4	$1,750,000	$203,400	_____

Market value = _____   7-5

FINANCIAL AND INVESTMENT ANALYSIS

In addition to an appraisal analysis to determine the current market value of a property, financial and investment analysis of an income-producing property is important. A thorough financial and investment analysis provides a better grasp of the probable future economic health of selected income-producing properties. As stated earlier, the discussion here will be limited to basic data required to conduct these analyses.

Five Forms of Income

Five forms of income must be dealt with in the analysis of income-producing property. The first three mentioned below were discussed earlier in this chapter in the income approach to estimating value.

1. *Potential gross income* (PGI): the total income a property would produce if 100% rented and no collection losses were incurred (the first step in a financial analysis).

2. *Effective gross income* (EGI): the actual income produced after vacancy and collection losses are subtracted from potential gross income and any income from sources other than rent (for example, laundry and vending machines) is added (the second step in financial analysis).

3. *Net operating income* (NOI): the income remaining after deducting all operating expenses from effective gross income. NOI is the annual income before mortgage or income-tax payments. It is the basis for the income approach in appraising as well as for financial and investment analysis.

    Potential Gross Income − Vacancy and Collection Losses
    + Other Income = Effective Gross Income

    Effective Gross Income − Operating Expenses = Net Operating Income

4. *Cash throwoff* (before-tax cash flow): the amount that results when annual debt service is subtracted from net operating income.

    Net Operating Income − Annual Debt Service Expense = Cash Throwoff

5. *Cash flow* (after-tax cash flow): the spendable income from an investment after deducting all operating expenses; cash throwoff minus income-tax liability. To calculate cash flow, begin with NOI and:

    a. Add back to NOI that amount of operating expenses allocated to "reserve for replacements."
    b. Subtract allowable depreciation and mortgage interest paid (but not mortgage principal). This then is "taxable income."
    c. Multiply taxable income by the investor's marginal tax rate to determine taxes due (or taxes saved).
    d. Add tax savings found to cash throwoff. Subtract any tax amount due from cash throwoff.
    e. Subtract all annual expenses for capital improvements (not repairs). The result at this point is cash flow (after-tax cash flow).

Predicting Future Return Rates and Economic Ratios

From estimates of an investment's income, expense, debt service and cash throwoff, several important rates and ratios can be calculated. Their primary purpose is to allow comparisons between alternative investment properties before purchase and to predict future rates of return to an investor. Rate of return calculations relate net operating income to capital investment in land and buildings.

Several terms, rates and ratios are involved in a thorough analysis of a real estate investment:

1. *Yield:* the percent of return an investor earns on the amount invested; a basic measurement of any investment's attractiveness.

2. *Equity dividend rate* (cash-on-cash return): the relationship between the amount of cash remaining after annual debt-service costs (mortgage payments) and invested capital.

$$\text{Equity Dividend Rate} = \frac{\text{Cash Throwoff}}{\text{Equity Invested}}$$

Example: The Citrus Apartment Building was purchased for $50,000 cash and a $200,000 mortgage at 12% for 30 years. Monthly mortgage payments are $2,057.24 (convert to an annual figure to agree with NOI: $2,057.24 × 12 months = $24,686.88). The property has a potential gross income of $126,200, an effective gross income of $117,900, and total operating expenses of $78,904, producing an NOI of $38,996 ($117,900 − $78,904). When the annual debt service is subtracted from the NOI ($38,996 − $24,686.88), the cash throwoff is $14,309.12. What is the equity dividend ratio?

$$\frac{\$14,309.12}{\$50,000.00} = .2861824 \text{ or } 28.6\% \text{ equity dividend rate}$$

Normally, equity dividend ratios range between 6% and 25%. The above hypothetical investor would be happy!

3. *Loan-to-value ratio* (LTV): the relationship between the amount borrowed and the appraised value (or purchase price) of a property; a measure of the financial risk associated with lending and borrowing money.

$$\text{Loan-to-Value Ratio} = \frac{\text{Loan Amount}}{\text{Value or Price}}$$

Example: What is the loan-to-value ratio for the Citrus Apartment Building example?

$$\frac{\$200,000}{\$250,000} = .80 \text{ or } 80\% \text{ loan-to-value ratio}$$

The normal range for LTV ratios is between 60% and 90%.

4. *Debt-service coverage ratio:* the relationship between net operating income and the mortgage payment; how much the NOI produced by a property can decrease and still meet the mortgage payment.

$$\text{Debt-Service Coverage Ratio} = \frac{\text{Net Operating Income}}{\text{Annual Mortgage Payment}}$$

Example: What is the debt-service coverage ratio for the Citrus Apartment Building?

$$\frac{\$38,996}{\$24,686.88} = 1.579624 \text{ or } 1.6 \text{ debt-service coverage ratio}$$

Lenders generally require a debt-service coverage ratio of at least 1.1. The higher the ratio, the more appealing the investment to both lender and investor.

5. *Operating expenses ratio:* the relationship between operating expenses and effective gross income.

$$\text{Operating Expenses Ratio} = \frac{\text{Operating Expenses}}{\text{Effective Gross Income}}$$

Example: What is the operating expense ratio for the Citrus Apartment Building?

$$\frac{\$78,904}{\$117,900} = .669245 \text{ or } 66.9\% \text{ operating expenses ratio}$$

The lower the ratio, the better it is for an investor.

6. *Cash breakeven ratio:* the relationship between total cash outlay costs and potential gross income.

$$\text{Cash Breakeven Ratio} = \frac{\begin{matrix}\text{Operating} & & \text{Reserve for} & & \text{Mortgage} \\ \text{Expenses} & - & \text{Replacements} & + & \text{Payment}\end{matrix}}{\text{Potential Gross Income}}$$

Example: If $5,772 of the operating expenses for the Citrus Apartment Building had been allocated to reserve for replacements, what would the cash breakeven ratio be for the property?

$$\frac{\$78,904 - \$5,772 + \$24,686.88}{\$126,200} = .77511 \text{ or } 77.5\% \text{ cash breakeven ratio}$$

A lower ratio would be more desirable to an investor. At 100%, expenses would equal income.

Practice: On March 1, an investor bought a 10-unit apartment building for $360,000. He paid $72,000 in cash and obtained a 30-year mortgage in the amount of $288,000. A review of the accounts over the preceding two years revealed that vacancy and collection losses were fairly stable at 4%. For the investor's 10 months of ownership during this calendar year, potential gross income for the property is $70,400 and the operating expenses are $12,770, including reserve for replacements of $2,812. Monthly mortgage payments are $2,742.71. Calculate the following:

Vacancy and collection losses $_____ (7-6)

Effective gross income $_____ (7-7)

Net operating income $_____ (7-8)

Debt-service cost $_____ (7-9)

Cash throwoff $_____ (7-10)

Equity dividend rate _____% (7-11)

Debt-service coverage ratio _____ (7-12)

Operating expense ratio _____% (7-13)

Cash breakeven ratio _____% (7-14)

CONSUMER PRICE INDEX (CPI)

The Consumer Price Index measures the average change in prices over time for a fixed "market basket" of goods and services. The results then provide a reliable indicator of inflation.

The current CPI is based on the average purchasing power of $1 during the period 1982 through 1984. (The previous CPI used 1967 as its "base year.") The base-year CPI is 100.0, and this means that the average index for the 1982–1984 period is regarded as 100% of exchange value. Or, put another way, it represents a full 100 cents of a dollar's purchasing power as a benchmark for measuring changes in prices. When the CPI increases, it is reflecting a rise in the overall price of consumer goods and services nationwide. For example, the CPI for January 1990 was 127.4, which was an increase in the cost of goods and services of 27.4% since 1982–1984. An increase in the CPI to 127.4, for example, indicates that about $1.28 was required in January 1990 to buy what $1 would have bought in 1982–1984.

Converting today's dollars to 1982–1984 dollars is necessary to determine if the dollars invested in real property have gained or lost in purchasing power. A higher price does not necessarily mean greater value! To determine if present-day dollars have gained or lost in purchasing power or exchange value, several details need to be mastered. The CPI is quoted as a three-digit number plus one digit after the decimal point (127.4, for example). Remember, however, that the CPI is expressed as a percentage. The decimal point must be moved two places to the left when solving problems. In addition, always divide the index number for the year of sale into the dollar amount of the sale price during that same year. For example, divide a 1990 index number (CPI) into a 1990 dollar amount. Never, for example, divide a 1982–1984 CPI into a 1990 dollar amount.

Example: You bought a house in 1985 for $78,000 when the CPI was 105.5. You sold it in 1989 for $89,500 when the CPI was 125.6. You made a profit of $11,500. Right? Yes and no! What actually happened to the exchange value of the dollars originally invested in the house?

First move the decimal point two places to the left in the 1985 CPI (1.055), and then divide that number into the 1985 purchase price to find the equivalent 1982–1984 dollars.

$$1982\text{–}1984 \text{ dollars} = \$78,000 \div 1.055 = \$73,933.65$$
$$= \$73,934 \text{ (rounded)}$$

Next move the decimal point two places to the left in the 1989 CPI (1.256), and then divide that number into the 1989 selling price to find the equivalent base period dollars.

$$1982\text{–}1984 \text{ dollars} = \$89,500 \div 1.256 = \$71,257.96$$
$$\$71,258 \text{ (rounded)}$$

What has happened to the purchasing power of the $78,000 you paid for your house in 1985?

```
1985 paid $78,000 = base period exchange value of $73,934
1989 sold $89,500 = base period exchange value of  71,258
                                                   $ 2,676
```

Despite the higher 1989 selling price, you actually lost $2,676 in exchange value (or purchasing power) between 1985 and 1989!

Practice: You sold a house to a customer for $51,400 in 1983. He had you sell the same house for him in 1989 for $62,000. The CPI in 1989 was 125.6. What has happened to the exchange value of the dollars paid for the house in 1983?

_____ 7-15

Note, however, that the above method to calculate gain or loss in real purchasing power approaches the situation from the viewpoint that both the purchase and the sale involved all cash. This is the traditional approach to calculating the effect of inflation as indicated by the CPI. But in real life, the vast majority of real estate transactions involve financing. The amount borrowed represents money that was not owned prior to the purchase, and in the case of residential purchases, it is paid back in monthly installments. Therefore, CPI calculations need to be separated into two distinct categories: the actual cash invested (down payment, cash at closing and closing costs) and the purchase-money mortgage (amount borrowed to complete the transaction).

Example: In 1985, you bought the same house described in the previous example for the same $78,000, including closing costs. However, you financed your purchase. You paid $7,700 cash plus $1,000 in closing costs for a total investment of $8,700. A conventional 30-year mortgage in the amount of $69,300 at 10% and a monthly payment of $608.18 provided the remainder of the purchase price. In 1989 when you sold your house for the same $89,500, the unpaid loan balance was $60,084. How has financing affected the exchange value of the home investment?

1982–1984 dollars actually invested in purchase:
$8,700 ÷ 1.055 = $8,246.45 or $8,246 (rounded)

Actual dollars received from the sale of the house:
$89,500 − $60,084 loan balance = $29,416

1982–1984 dollars = $29,416 ÷ 1.256= $23,420.38 or
= $23,420 (rounded)

What has happened to the purchasing power of the original home investment?

1989 dollars received converted to 1982–1984 dollars = $23,420
1985 dollars invested converted to 1982–1984 dollars =   8,246
A gain in purchasing power of: $15,174

The authors consider this last-described method to be a more typical and accurate procedure for solving CPI problems; however, it is not a universally accepted method. Many knowledgeable professionals use the all-cash transaction approach.

Practice: In 1983, you sold a new house to a customer for $66,700, including buyer's closing costs. The customer used FHA financing to obtain a loan in the amount of $63,850 and paid $2,850 in cash as her total investment. In 1988 when the CPI was 115.7, you sold the same house for your principal for $89,200. The unpaid balance of the existing mortgage was $61,454.

What was the dollar amount of the base period (1982–1984) purchasing power invested in the house?

_____ 7-16

What was the dollar amount of the base period purchasing power represented by the selling price?

_____ 7-17

How much did the real purchasing power of the dollars invested in the house increase or decrease?

_____ 7-18

REVIEW PROBLEMS

What is the economic life or the annual rate of depreciation in the following situations?

	Economic Life of Building	Annual Rate of Depreciation
1.	30 years	—%
2.	— years	4%
3.	— years	5%
4.	35 years	—%
5.	45 years	—%

6. A house has an effective age of 12 years and an annual depreciation rate of 2%. The cost to reproduce the house new is $76,000. What is the current value of the house?

_____

7. An office building was given a useful life of 40 years when new. The depreciated value of the building with an effective age of 7 years is $148,500. What is the cost to reproduce the building?

_____

8. The remaining current value of a 10-year-old triplex has been appraised at $66,000. The cost to reproduce the triplex is $82,500. What is the annual rate of depreciation?

_____

9. What is the accrued depreciation rate for a 12-year-old duplex that had an economic life of 50 years when new?

_____

10. A 6-year-old laundry building is currently valued at $92,000. A useful life of 40 years was given the building when new. What percent of the building's cost of reproduction applies to the building currently?

_____

11. A house cost $89,500 to build. A 50-year useful life was assigned the house when new. What is the amount of depreciation after 4 years?

_____

12. As part of appraising a vacant residential lot, you have located four comparable lot sales. If the subject lot is 125 feet by 150 feet, what is the market value as derived from the four sales? Consider all sales equal regarding location, time and physical characteristics.

Sale	Size	Sale Price
1	130′ × 150′	$11,900
2	120′ × 150′	$11,700
3	110′ × 130′	$ 8,300
4	140′ × 140′	$11,760

_____

13. A small apartment building earns $14,000 net income per year. A knowledgeable investor requires at least a 12½% rate of return on her investment. What is the most the investor should pay for this property?

_____

14. The outline below shows the foundation perimeter of a single-story house with a useful life of 40 years. What is the number of square feet in the house?

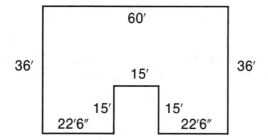

_____

15. The house in problem 14 can be reproduced today for $48 per square foot. What will the cost be to reproduce it new?

_____

16. Using the data from problems 14 and 15, what is the appraised value of the property if the lot is valued at $18,000 and the house is 4 years old?

_____

17. In 1986 when the CPI was 109.6, Mr. Pinellas bought a house for $69,900 cash. In 1988 when the CPI was 120.5, Mr. Pinellas sold his house for $78,000. How much has the purchasing power of the original dollars invested increased? (Round to the nearest dollar.)

_____

18. You are appraising a rental house and have collected data from four comparable sales to establish a monthly gross rent multiplier. What will the MGRM be?

Sale	Sale Price	Monthly Rental	MGRM
1	$61,100	$470	_____
2	$62,225	$475	_____
3	$61,180	$460	_____
4	$60,970	$455	_____

_____

19. The rental house you are appraising has been renting for $470 per month. On the basis of the monthly gross rent multiplier developed in problem 18, what is the value of the rental house?

_____

20. A 2-year-old apartment house would cost $134,000 to reproduce new. It had an estimated economic life of 50 years when new. The site on which the building stands is valued at $25,000. A check of the owner's operating statement shows an annual net income of $21,500. If you must have a 14% rate of return on your investment, what is the maximum you can pay for the apartment house and realize your 14% rate of return?

_____

21. What would the total current value be of the apartment house and land in problem 20 based on the cost-depreciation approach to value?

_____

22. A property has total operating expenses of $180,000, of which $5,000 is reserve for replacements. Annual debt service is $165,000 and potential gross income is $400,000. What is the cash breakeven ratio for this property?

_____

Chapter 8

Prorating for Closing Statements

After the signing of a contract for the sale/purchase of real property, actual transfer of ownership is usually concluded at a "closing." A written statement of expenses and income must be prepared before the official closing (the "settlement date"). Before this can be done, a number of computations are required to determine the expenses and income to be included on the "closing statement."

No attempt will be made here to cover the "how" and "why" involved in the preparation of a complete closing statement. The main objective of this chapter is to explain and illustrate how to determine the expenses and income that must be shown on the closing statement.

PRORATING

To "prorate" means to divide or share proportionately. On closing statements, the income and expenses associated with the transaction are divided between the seller and the buyer according to the time each party has owned, or will own, the property.

Each prorating problem usually involves finding answers to one or more of the following related questions:

1. Who owes whom?

2. For what period of time?

3. How much is owed?

Each prorated item, when computed, will be shown as either a "debit" (charge) or a "credit" to each party. It may be helpful to regard the terms debit and credit as simply headings for columns of data. Under the heading "debit" are included amounts that are owed at closing. Under the heading "credit" are included amounts that are to be received at closing. These terms apply to both buyer and seller when prorating. For example, if the buyer owes the seller $50, the buyer is debited $50 and the seller is credited $50. If the seller owes the buyer $50, the seller is debited $50 and the buyer is credited $50.

For ease in calculating, proration problems in this book will be solved by ending the seller's ownership rights as of midnight prior to the closing date (day), unless indicated otherwise. In some locations, sellers' ownership interests end on midnight of the closing date. In other words, the sales contract should specify whether prorations are to be "to" the date of closing or "through" the date of closing. This, then, makes it clear to whom the day of closing is assigned.

Prorating is usually required when rent is paid in advance, when property taxes are paid in arrears, when hazard insurance is paid in advance and when interest on mortgages is either overdue or prepaid.

Three methods of prorating income and expenses are commonly used.

        1. 30-day month method

        2. Average month-day method

        3. 365-day method

While the 365-day method is the most accurate (366 days in a leap year), any one of the three methods may be specified as the one to use for a particular problem situation.

Procedure: 30-Day Month Method

In this method, all months are considered to have 30 days. In those states in which this method is used for prorating (sometimes called the "360-day statutory year method"), the period of time in question is calculated by a simple subtraction process, called the "subtraction-of-dates method."

Numbers are used for each year, month and day, and they must be written in that order. Always subtract the earlier date from the later date. Begin by subtracting on the right side (days) and move to the left. If the days will not subtract, "borrow" an entire 30-day month from the month column. If the months will not subtract, borrow an entire year (12 months) from the year column and conclude by subtracting the remaining years.

Example: A three-year hazard insurance policy cost $712.80 when taken out and was prepaid by the homeowner. Determine the time period remaining from September 26, 1989 through the expiration date (midnight, February 16, 1992).

	Year	Month	Day
		13	
	1	1̸	46
February 16, 1992:	199̸2	2̸	1̸6̸
September 26, 1989:	1989	9	26
	2	4	20

Thus, the time interval in question is 2 years, 4 months, 20 days.

Using the above time period, prorate to find the insurance amount that the buyer will owe the homeowner/seller.

Yearly cost: $712.80 ÷ 3 years = $237.60
Monthly cost: $237.60 ÷ 12 months = $19.80
Daily cost: $19.80 ÷ 30 days = $.66

   Yearly cost: $237.60 × 2 years = $475.20
   Monthly cost: $19.80 × 4 months =   79.20
   Daily cost: $.66 × 20 days   = + 13.20
                                 $567.60

Thus, the buyer will owe the seller $567.60 for the insurance remaining.

Procedure: Average Month-Day Method

This method of prorating is also called the "actual-days-in-the-month method." First, the annual amount is divided by the number of months in a year, then the monthly amount is divided by the actual number of days in the closing month.

Annual cost or income ÷ 12 months = average monthly cost or income

Average monthly cost or income ÷ number of days in the closing month = average daily cost or income

Total months' cost or income + total days' cost or income = total prorated cost or income

Example: Closing day is June 15. The annual insurance premium is $180 and has been paid by the seller. How much is the buyer to pay the seller for the prepaid insurance remaining if the policy is to expire at midnight on November 30?

$180 ÷ 12 months = $15 per month
$15 ÷ 30 days (in June) = $.50 per day

The buyer will receive insurance coverage for 5 complete months (July through November) and 16 days in June.

$15 per month × 5 months = $75
$.50 per day × 16 days = $8
$75 + $8 = $83 (credit to seller, debit to buyer)

Note that the month of closing (June) had 30 days. Therefore, the average monthly cost was divided by 30 to find the average daily cost. The average monthly cost would have been divided by 31 days if the month of closing had been July, or 28 days if February, and so on.

Do not forget to add any odd number of days in a month when insurance expires on some day other than the last day. In the above example, if the insurance policy had expired on November 9 instead of November 30, a total time of 4 months and 25 days (July through October and 16 days in June plus 9 days in November) would have resulted.

Practice: Closing date is April 20. A homeowner's insurance policy has been prepaid one year in advance at a cost of $162. The policy expiration date is midnight, December 12. How much will the buyer owe to the seller for prepaid insurance transferred?

_____ 8-1

Procedure: 365-Day Method

There are two approaches to using the 365-day (366 days in a leap year) method. The most common procedure is:

Total cost or income ÷ 365 days = daily cost or income

Daily cost or income × total days transferred = prorated cost or income

Example: Refer to the June 15 closing example on the previous page.

$180 ÷ 365 days = $.4931506 per day

The exact number of days remaining in the insurance policy = June 15–30; July 1–31; August 1–31, September 1–30; October 1–31; and, November 1–30. Total number of days remaining = 169.

169 days × $.4931506 = $83.342451
= $83.34 (rounded)

In some states, a different procedure is used to prorate with the 365-day method.

(Exact number of days ÷ 365 days) × total cost = prorated cost

Example: Again refer to the June 15 closing example.

(169 days ÷ 365 days) × $180 =
.4630136 × $180 = $83.342448
= $83.34 (rounded)

Whenever prorating, always consider whether the expense involved is paid in advance (as with homeowner's insurance) or paid in arrears (as with taxes). Who will be charged (debited) and who will be credited will be determined by this property consideration.

Example: Consider a transaction scheduled to close on July 15 of a 365-day year. Taxes for the year are estimated to be $986 and are to be prorated between seller and buyer. Who owes whom and how much?

As taxes are normally paid at the end of the year, the taxes have not yet been paid. The seller owes the buyer for the seller's period of ownership.

$986 ÷ 365 days = $2.7013698 per day
$2.7013698 × 195 days (Jan. 1 through July 14) =
$526.76711 or $526.77 (rounded). Seller owes buyer $526.77.

On the closing statement, the seller will be debited $526.77 and the buyer will be credited $526.77.

Whichever prorating procedure is used should reflect the actual number of days a property was owned by the seller and will be owned by the buyer. Because of the need to know the actual number of days involved when prorating income and expenses, it is a good idea to use some technique for remembering the number of days in each month. Some people memorize this simple little poem:

30 days has September,
April, June and November
All the rest have 31,
Except February with only 28
(but in leap year, 29).

Other people prefer to use the "fist method" for remembering the number of days in a month. Make each hand into a fist as seen below. Begin with the knuckle of the little finger on your left hand, which will be named January, and move from left to right assigning the names of the month to each knuckle and each valley as follows:

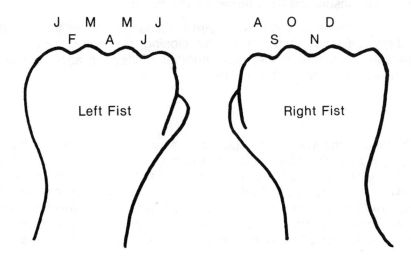

Note that all knuckles represent 31-day months, even July and August, both of which have 31 days. The valleys between the knuckles represent 30-day months, except for February, which everyone remembers has only 28 (29 in a leap year).

Example: If a closing is scheduled for July 20 of a 365-day year, taxes should be allocated as follows:

Days:	31	28	31	30	31	30	31	31	30	31	30	31
Month:	J	F	M	A	M	J	J	A	S	O	N	D
Owned:			Seller: 200 days						Buyer: 165 days			

July
20

Practice: How many days are represented by the following periods of time in 365-day years?

January 1 to midnight March 6: _____ days 8-2

December 21 to midnight July 29: _____ days 8-3

March 4 to midnight August 17: _____ days 8-4

Note: For all problems that follow in this chapter (examples, practice and review), the more accurate 365- (366-) day method of proration will be used (total cost or income ÷ number of days in period × number of days "owned").

PRORATING PROPERTY INSURANCE

Hazard or homeowner's insurance policies are normally written to cover one or more years. Insurance premiums are payable in advance. This requires the buyer to reimburse the seller for any unused insurance transferred to the buyer.

If the precise number of days is required, calculate the exact number of days by counting the days remaining in the month of closing, beginning with the day the buyer assumes ownership, and adding the exact number of days in each month up to but not including the anniversary date of the policy.

Example: On June 1, the Maloneys bought a two-year homeowner's policy that insured 80 percent of their home, which was appraised at $185,000. That December they sold their home, and the buyers assumed the remainder of the existing insurance policy, which had cost $.36 per $100 of insured value per annum. The closing date of February 28 was assigned to the sellers. How much is owed to whom for the prorated remainder of the homeowner's insurance? (Both the average month-day and 365-day methods—no leap years involved—are shown.)

> $185,000 appraised value $\times$ .80 = $148,000 insured value
> $148,000 insured value $\div$ $100 = 1,480
> 1,480 $\times$ $.36 = $532.80 annual cost of insurance policy

Insurance remaining: From March 1 of the year of closing through May 31 of the following year:

> March 1 through December 31 = 10 months or 306 days
> January 1 through May 31   = 5 months or 151 days
> _____
> 15 months or 457 days

Average month-day method:
> $532.80 insurance cost $\div$ 12 months = $44.40 per month
> $44.40 $\times$ 15 months = $666 buyers owe sellers

365-day method:
> $532.80 insurance cost $\div$ 365 days = $1.4597, or $1.46 per day
> $1.46 $\times$ 457 days = $667.22 buyers owe sellers

Practice: A 3-year insurance policy was purchased on April 3, 1989 at a cost of $1,314. The insured property was sold and the closing was held on June 1, 1990. The unused portion of the insurance was transferred to the buyer. How should the cost of insurance be prorated on the closing statement, and what amount is involved?

> Debit the _____ $ _____
>
> Credit the _____ $ _____

8-5

PRORATING PROPERTY TAXES

Unless a transaction is closed on January 1 or the first day of the tax year, property taxes always must be prorated.

Property taxes are usually paid in arrears at the end of the tax year. If taxes have not been assessed at the time of closing, the most recent tax information is used as a basis for computation. If taxes have not been paid for the year in which the closing occurs, the seller will owe the buyer for the seller's period of ownership up to midnight prior to the closing date.

To determine the correct amount of time involved and to convert the time into dollars, the following procedure is used:

Annual taxes ÷ 365 (or 366) days = daily tax cost
Daily tax cost × days of ownership = prorated tax cost

Example: The closing date for a transaction was May 12. The tax year runs from January 1 through December 31. The estimated taxes are $1,168. How should the taxes be prorated?

$1,168 ÷ 365 days = $3.20 daily tax cost

The seller owned the property up to midnight May 11, or 131 days. His taxes will be paid at the end of the year by the buyer. But the seller has to pay his portion at closing.

$3.20 × 131 days = $419.20 (due buyer from seller)

Debit seller $419.20
Credit buyer $419.20

Practice: Closing will be on October 16. Estimated taxes are $876, and your broker has asked you to tell the buyer and the seller what each will owe or receive credit for at closing. How will you allocate the property taxes?

Debit _____ $ _____

Credit _____ $ _____

8-6

PRORATING RENT

Normally, any rent collected in advance belongs to the new owner, beginning with the date of closing. Thus, the total rent amount is divided and allocated as follows:

Total rent ÷ number of days in rental period =

average rent per day

Average rent per day × days owned = prorated share

Example: Assume that a property rents for $475 per month. The closing date is on the 21st day of a 31-day month. The proration would be as follows:

$475 ÷ 31 days = $15.32258 per day

$15.32258 × 11 days = $168.54838, or rounds to
= $168.55 due buyer from seller

This exact amount involved must be accounted for on the closing statement. Since the seller has already collected the rent in advance, the seller will owe the buyer (debit the seller $168.55; credit the buyer $168.55).

Practice: The sale of a duplex will be closed on December 12. The seller collected the rent for December amounting to $548 on December 1. How should the rent be prorated on the closing statement? Show who will be debited and credited and for how much.

Debit the _____ $ _____

8-7

Credit the _____ $ _____

PRORATING MORTGAGE INTEREST

Since mortgage payments are normally made each month, the period for calculating interest prorations is usually one month. Unless otherwise stated, mortgages are written so that interest is paid in arrears (after having use of the money). Thus, the seller is debited (charged) up to midnight prior to the closing date and the buyer is credited for that period, with the buyer being responsible for the closing date and thereafter.

When solving problems dealing with interest in arrears, first determine the correct number of days allocated to the seller. Then convert those days into dollars and, unless directed otherwise, debit the seller and credit the buyer.

When the amount of interest must be determined before the interest can be prorated, use the following procedure (similar to that found in the Mortgage Math chapter):

Mortgage amount $\times$ interest rate $\div$ 12 months = month's interest

Month's interest $\div$ days in month = daily interest

Daily interest $\times$ days interest is owed = prorated interest

Example: A closing is scheduled for March 20, 1991. The buyer will assume the seller's existing mortgage of $63,500 at 11% interest, which is paid up to and including February 25, 1991. The next mortgage payment is due March 26, 1991. How will the mortgage interest be prorated on the closing statement?

Days in month (Feb. 26 through March 25):
Feb. 26 to March 1	3 days
March 1 to March 26	25 days
	28 days of interest

Days interest owed by seller:
Feb. 26 to March 1	3 days
March 1 to March 20	19 days
	22 days of interest owed by seller

$63,500 $\times$ 11% $\div$ 12 months = $582.08333 month's interest

$582.08333 $\div$ 28 days = $20.78869 daily interest

$20.78869 $\times$ 22 days = $457.35 (debit seller, credit buyer)

Prorating interest paid in advance by the seller is handled exactly as prorating interest in arrears, except that the buyer owes the seller for the period that is transferred to the buyer.

Practice: The sale of a house is to be closed on August 12. The buyer will assume the existing mortgage of $40,000 at 9-3/4% interest. The buyer is to make the next payment on September 1. The last payment made by the seller paid the interest up to but not including August 1. How should the mortgage interest be prorated on the closing statement?

Debit _____ $ _____

Credit _____ $ _____

8-8

ORGANIZING THE INFORMATION

To compute the many individual amounts that are entered on a closing statement, a considerable number of calculations must be made. It is always a good idea to use some type of worksheet to collect and organize the results of these computations.

For this purpose, a copy of the authors' "Work Organizer for Closing Statements" is provided immediately following the review problems at the end of this chapter. As individual results are computed in the lower portions of the form, they may be written in the appropriate space(s) in the upper portions for subsequent use.

Note 1   (The three sections from left to right at the very bottom of the Organizer dealing with tax stamps may or may not be applicable in your state.)

Note 2   (The assignment of debits and credits may vary from area to area and from transaction to transaction because all items are theoretically negotiable.)

Notice that there is space provided for all of the subject areas covered earlier in this book. When the time to prepare a formal closing statement arrives (see Composite Closing Statement form), it becomes a simple routine of extracting data from the Organizer.

As mentioned in the opening paragraph of this chapter, the aim has been to help you improve your ability to perform the many math computations necessary to determine the income and expenses to be included on a closing statement. The aim has *not* been to teach you how to prepare and balance a formal closing statement.

Finally, the purpose of the entire book has been to help you with the math related to real estate, *not* to teach you the principles, practices and laws of real estate.

REVIEW PROBLEMS

1. You sold a house for $80,000. The buyer made an earnest money deposit of $5,000 and will assume an existing FHA mortgage with an unpaid balance of $50,000 at 11-1/2% interest. The seller has agreed to take back a new second mortgage of $15,000 with the remainder of the purchase price to be paid at closing, which is scheduled for May 16. The buyer is to pay the taxes created by the second mortgage, and the seller is to pay the taxes associated with the deed. The property has been rented during the past year, and advance rent of $480 was collected by the seller for the month of May. The seller has paid $198 for a one-year insurance policy that became effective January 22. Property taxes have been estimated at $1,095 for the year. The last payment made on the mortgage paid the interest up to and including April 30.

Using the information from this and previous chapters, solve the following problems (assume a 365-day year and use the tax rates provided at the bottom of page 131):

	Prorations	Debit/Credit Buyer/Seller		Amount
a.	Insurance	Debit _____	Credit _____	$ _____
b.	Taxes	Debit _____	Credit _____	$ _____
c.	Rent	Debit _____	Credit _____	$ _____
d.	Interest	Debit _____	Credit _____	$ _____

	Expenses	Debit Buyer/Seller	Amount
e.	Documentary stamps (deed)	_____	$ _____
f.	Documentary stamps (note)	_____	$ _____
g.	Intangible tax (mortgage)	_____	$ _____

2. Mr. Hernando has signed a purchase contract to buy a small apartment building. The purchase price is $110,000, with the closing set for June 10. Mr. Hernando will assume the seller's FHA mortgage, which has an unpaid balance of $70,300. The seller, Ms. Clay, has agreed to take back a new second mortgage in the amount of $28,000 with Mr. Hernando to pay the taxes related to the new mortgage. Ms. Clay will pay the taxes on the deed (use the tax rates provided at the bottom of page 131). Other contractural agreements are as follows: (a 365-day year applies)

Binder deposit: $11,700.
First mortgage interest: $565.50 in arrears (for the period June 1 through 30).
Property taxes: city, school, district and county taxes combined estimated to be $3,294 for the year.
Insurance: $2,190 paid by Ms. Clay for a 3-year policy effective March 1 of this year. Mr. Hernando will purchase Ms. Clay's unused portion.
Rent: $1,710 collected in advance for the period June 1 through 30.
Deed: warranty deed to be delivered with all required stamps paid.

	Prorations	Debit/Credit Buyer/Seller	Amount
a.	Insurance	Debit _____ Credit _____	$ _____
b.	Taxes	Debit _____ Credit _____	$ _____
c.	Rent	Debit _____ Credit _____	$ _____
d.	Interest	Debit _____ Credit _____	$ _____

	Expenses	Debit Buyer/Seller	Amount
e.	Documentary stamps (deed)	_____	$ _____
f.	Documentary stamps (note)	_____	$ _____
g.	Intangible tax (mortgage)	_____	$ _____

Work Organizer for Closing Statements

DEBIT BUYER	CREDIT BUYER	DEBIT SELLER	CREDIT SELLER
Purchase Price $ ____	Deposit $ ____ 1st Mortgage ____ 2nd Mortgage ____ Prorated: ____	1st Mortgage $ ____ 2nd Mortgage ____ Doc. Stamps on Deed ____	Purchase Price $ ____
Prorated Ins. ____ 1st Mortgage ____ 2nd Mortgage ____ Doc. Stamps on Note ____	City Taxes ____ County Taxes ____ Rent ____ Mort. Int. ____ Security Deposit ____	Abstract ____ Intang. Tax on Mortgage ____ Prorated: City Taxes ____	Prorated Ins. ____ 1st Mortgage ____ 2nd Mortgage ____
Intang. Tax on Mortgage ____	TOTAL CREDITS $ ____	County Taxes ____ Rent ____ Mort. Int. ____	TOTAL CREDITS $ ____
Atty. Fees ____	Total Debits $ ____	Atty. Fees ____ Record Mort. ____	Total Credits $ ____
Record Deed ____	less	Commission ____	less
Title Ins. ____ TOTAL BUYER DEBITS $ ____	Total Credits ____ DUE FROM BUYER $ ____	Miscellaneous ____ TOTAL SELLER DEBITS $ ____	Total Debits ____ BALANCE DUE SELLER $ ____

INSURANCE	CITY TAXES	COUNTY TAXES
Premium cost $\div$ 365 = daily cost Daily cost $\times$ no. of days to Buyer (DEBIT BUYER; CREDIT SELLER)	Annual taxes $\div$ 365 = daily cost Daily cost $\times$ no. of days used by Seller (DEBIT SELLER; CREDIT BUYER)	Annual taxes $\div$ 365 = daily cost Daily cost $\times$ no. of days used by Seller (DEBIT SELLER; CREDIT BUYER)

PREPAID RENT	1st MORTGAGE INTEREST	COMMISSION
Amt./period $\div$ days in period Days owned by Buyer _____ $\times$ amount per day _____ (DEBIT SELLER; CREDIT BUYER)	Balance due $\times$ % = annual int. Annual int. $\div$ 12 = month's int. Month's int. $\div$ days in month = Daily int. $\times$ no. of days used	Purchase price $ ____ $\times$ ____ %

DOC. STAMPS DEED	DOC. STAMPS NOTE	INTANG. TAX MORT.	MISCELLANEOUS
$.55 $\times$ $100 on purchase price	$.32 $\times$ $100 on note face value	.002 (mills) $\times$ $1 mort. face val.	

For practice, use the actual tax rates in effect for your state.

Note: The debiting/crediting of all items may vary and is negotiable.

Closing date: Month _____ Day _____ Year _____ ("charged" to _____)
Method of prorating: _____

COMPOSITE CLOSING STATEMENT

SELLER'S STATEMENT   BUYER'S STATEMENT

Debit	Credit	Item	Debit	Credit
		Total purchase price		
		Binder deposit		
		First mortgage - balance		
		Second mortgage		
		Prorations & Prepayments:		
		Rent		
		Interest - first mortgage		
		Interest - second mortgage		
		Prepayment - first mortgage		
		Prepayment - second mortgage		
		Insurance		
		Taxes - city		
		Taxes - county		
		Other:		
		Expenses:		
		Abstract continuation		
		Attorney's fees		
		Title insurance		
		Brokerage commission		
		Documentary Stamps:		
		Mortgage - Note		
		State on deed		
		Intangible tax - mortgage		
		Recording:		
		Mortgage		
		Deed		
		Miscellaneous:		
		TOTAL - DEBITS & CREDITS		
		BALANCE DUE TO SELLER · BALANCE DUE FROM BUYER		
		GRAND TOTALS		

BROKER'S STATEMENT

	Receipts	Disbursements
Binder deposit	_____	_____
Check from buyer at closing	_____	_____
Brokerage commission	_____	_____
Check to seller at closing	_____	_____
Seller's expense (less brokerage)	_____	_____
Buyer's expense	_____	_____
TOTALS:	_____	_____

Post-Tests

The following *two* practice examinations are representative of the types of math problems which may appear on an actual examination. All of the math involved has been covered in this book. If appropriate, use a calculator.

POST-TEST "A"

1. A house was listed by your employer at $105,000. You sold the house for 95% of the list price. How much did the buyer pay for the house? $ _____

2. A two-acre lot is 330′ deep. How wide is it? _____ feet

3. Your business records reveal that it takes you an average of 10 showings to sell a house. You have analyzed your cost to show houses and have found that $25 is the average cost to show a house one time. Your broker retains four-sevenths of the 7% sales commission charged for selling residential properties. If you sell a house for $60,000 under average conditions, what is your net pretax income from the sale? $ _____

4. The monthly payment for principal and interest on a $64,500 loan at 11-1/2% for 30 years is $638.75. What amount of the second month's payment will be paid on the unpaid principal? $ _____

5. The street in front of your house is to be paved at a cost of $35 per running foot. The city has agreed to pay 30% of the paving cost and will assess abutting properties for the remainder. If your lot frontage on that street is 75 feet, what will be the cost of your portion of the special assessment? $ _____

6. At the expiration of a loan period of 18 months, a broker paid his bank a total of $20,565, which included $2,565 interest. What was the interest rate? _____%

7. A developer bought half of a quarter section of land for $160,000. Existing zoning in that area requires all lots to be no smaller than 100′ × 120′. The developer has allocated 484,800 square feet of the tract to streets, sidewalks and recreation areas. Development costs for utilities, streets and other amenities will amount to five times the amount paid for the land. The developer calculates his total costs and adds 10% for his profit. How much will each lot sell for to accomplish the developer's profit objective? $ _____

8. How many acres are contained in the following legal description: "The NE¼ of the SE¼ and the SE¼ of the NE¼ and the N½ of the NE¼"? _____acres

9. Between 1965 and 1990, the population of a metropolitan area increased from 200,000 to 346,000, an increase of what percent? _____ %

10. The cost per sq. ft. of an $18,000 lot is $1.50; the area is _____ sq. ft.

11. A real estate investor has $150,000 to invest in income-producing property. She is looking for a return of 15% on her money. What must a property produce as net income in order to attract this investor? $ _____

12. What will the cost per acre be of a parcel that sold for $697,500 and is described as: "That tract beginning at a point on the North side of State Highway 1, exactly 200 feet West of the corner formed by the intersection of the West boundary of Clementine Way and the North boundary of State Highway 1; thence running due West (N90°W) 4,000 feet to a concrete marker; thence due North (N00°E) 2,000 feet to a concrete marker; thence due East (S90°E) 2,534 feet to a concrete marker; thence directly (S39°E) to the point of beginning."

_____ per acre

13. A small apartment building contains three apartments that are all leased and occupied. Apartment #1 is 32' × 35½' and rents for $3,960 per year; Apartment #2 is 30' × 40' and rents for $300 per month; and Apartment #3 is 24' × 36' and rents for $70 per week. What is the average annual income per square foot? $ _____ /sq. ft.

14. A parcel of land is utilized in fractional parts as follows: 2/5 is leased to a car rental agency; 25% is leased to a nearby business for parking; and the remaining 9,800 square feet is leased by a miniature golf course. What is the total area of the parcel? _____ square feet

15. A contractor borrowed $38,000 at 10% interest for 30 months. At the end of the period, he paid back the borrowed amount plus all uncompounded interest in one payment. What amount was the single payment? $ _____

16. What is the gross rent multiplier for a house that sold for $42,900 and rents for $390?

_____

17. A home sold for $76,700 with FHA 30-year, fixed-rate financing at 9½% interest. The maximum FHA-insured loan amount in that area was $78,800. The FHA mortgage discount was 3 points. The property was assessed at 95% of the sale price, and the total tax rate was 29 mills. What was the:

    Cost of the mortgage discount points? $ _____

    Real yield to the lender? _____%

    Annual property tax amount? $ _____

18. In 1986 when the CPI was 109.6, you bought a house for $82,400 (which included the sale price plus closing costs). Your total investment consisted of a $2,000 down payment, $9,100 cash at closing and $900 closing costs. You arranged a 30-year conventional loan at 10.75% in the amount of $70,400 to conclude the transaction. Monthly payments were $657.18. In 1990 when the CPI was 126.8, you sold your house for $129,000. The unpaid balance of the mortgage was $68,379. How much did the exchange value (purchasing power) of your original home investment increase or decrease between 1986 and 1990? $ _____ increase/decrease (cross out one)

• Use the following information for <u>questions 19 and 20</u>:

    A house sold for $69,800 with the closing on June 15. An existing mortgage with an unpaid balance of $51,250 at 9¾% was assumed by the buyers. Monthly payments are paid in arrears in the amount of $532.68 for principal and interest. Principal and interest were paid up to, but not including, June 1. Property taxes were $1,110 for the previous year. The seller bought a one-year hazard insurance policy for $146, effective March 2 of the current year. The property has been rented for two years for $505 per month. The seller collected the June rent in advance. (365-day years apply)

19. Prorate the rent, taxes and insurance.

	Debit	**Credit**	**Amount**
Rent:	_____	_____	$ _____
Taxes:	_____	_____	$ _____
Insurance:	_____	_____	$ _____

20. Calculate the interest for June and allocate it correctly.

    Debit _____ $ _____

    Credit _____ $ _____

POST-TEST "B"

1. The Northwest ¼ of the Northeast ¼ of the Southwest ¼, Section 20, Township 4 South, Range 2 East, describes a tract of:

   a. 64 acres.
   b. 10 acres.
   c. .5 acre.
   d. .125 acre.

2. An owner of an office building lists her building for sale with the stipulation that she must net $216,000 from the sale. If tax stamps and other closing costs amount to $3,200 and the listing agreement allows a 10% sales commission, what should the legitimate, ethical selling price be?

   a. $240,000
   b. $240,800
   c. $243,200
   d. $243,556

3. A buyer has made a down payment of $10,150 on a house selling for $94,500. A local thrift institution has agreed to lend 85% of the selling price at 10½% interest for 30 years. If the buyer's closing costs amount to $1,575, how much more cash must the buyer produce at closing?

   a. $ 5,600
   b. $ 7,175
   c. $12,889
   d. $14,175

4. An undeveloped tract of land has 2,080 feet of highway frontage with a perpendicular boundary measuring 2,095 feet. The property is triangular-shaped and has been sold for $4,000 per acre. Rounding the tract acreage to the nearest acre, the sale price is:

   a. $ 50,000.
   b. $100,000.
   c. $200,000.
   d. $400,000.

5. Mr. and Mrs. Duval bought an undeveloped 10-acre tract for $5,000 per acre. They built a $100,000 house on the land. Two years later, they sold the entire property. The house sold for $34,000 more than it cost, and the land had doubled in value. Disregarding closing costs and other expenses, what was the percent of profit?

   a. 36 percent
   b. 42 percent
   c. 56 percent
   d. 64 percent

6. A builder borrowed $72,000 to build a house. He agreed to pay $2,160 per quarter in interest until the house was sold. From the sale of the house, he is to pay the entire loan principal in one lump sum. The annual interest rate of the loan is:

   a. 6 percent.
   b. 9 percent.
   c. 12 percent.
   d. 15 percent.

7. A farmer decides to lease part of his land. He agrees to an annual lease rate of $150 per acre to be paid for fully usable land only. The leased tract measures 600' × 1,815' and has a required drainage pond within its boundaries. The drainage pond is 120 feet wide and 726 feet long. How many acres of usable land are available for lease, and what amount will the farmer receive under the terms cited?

   _____ acres available
   $ _____ received by farmer

8. A land sales mortgage contract requires monthly payments of $500. The first month's interest amounted to $400, with the balance of the monthly payment applied to reduction of principal. If the annual rate of interest is 10%, what was the original amount of the loan?

   a. $40,000
   b. $48,000
   c. $53,333
   d. $60,000

9. A brokerage firm lists a small office building for $225,000. The broker agrees to a graduated sales commission rate of 5% on the first $50,000 of the sale price, 6% on the next $100,000, and 10% of any balance. A salesman sold the property for $220,000. From the total sales commission received, the broker paid the listing salesperson 20% and divided the remainder of the sales commission evenly between himself and the salesperson who sold the property. What was the total sales commission received by the brokerage firm? $ _____
   What amount did the listing salesperson receive? $ _____
   What amount did the selling salesperson receive? $ _____

Use the following information for questions 10 through 15:

On July 5, you showed a home to Mr. and Mrs. Dave Maybuy. The house was listed at $79,500. The original owners, Mr. and Mrs. George Duwrite, had an existing mortgage with interest paid to, but not including, July 1 and an unpaid balance of $54,460 for 30 years. Twenty-eight years remain of the entire loan term, and the mortgage can be assumed. The owners recently bought a 3-year homeowner's insurance policy for $552 with coverage beginning March 12 of this same year. The Duwrites were willing to take back a second mortgage as part of the purchase agreement; however, they insisted on at least 10% of the purchase price in cash by the closing date. The lot on which the house is located is rectangular in shape and measures 110' x 120'. It is well landscaped and probably contributed to the property's $71,700 assessed valuation. As the broker, you know the tax rate for that community was set at 29.86 mills last year. More recent tax information is not available. Taxes are payable for the period January 1 through December 31 each year and have not been paid for the current year.

Mr. and Mrs. Maybuy liked the house and lot. They made an offer of $78,000, but the offer was contingent on all appliances remaining in place and a second mortgage in the amount of $26,000 at 12% per annum for 15 years. They included a $2,000 check as an earnest money deposit.

The Duwrites made a counteroffer at $78,900. They agreed to leave the appliances but restricted the second mortgage to $15,540 at 12% for 10 years. The balance of the purchase price is to be paid at closing after the Maybuys assume the existing mortgage. All expenses created by the new second mortgage are to be paid by the Maybuys, who agreed to the terms of the counteroffer.

Closing was set for July 20. An inquiry at the local mortgage lender's office disclosed that the amount of interest due on August 1, for the month of July, was $544.60 and is to be prorated as of midnight prior to closing.

Prorate the property taxes, homeowner's insurance and mortgage interest (use 365-day years):

		Debit	Credit	Amount
10.	Taxes:	_____	_____	$ _____
11.	Insurance:	_____	_____	$ _____
12.	Interest:	_____	_____	$ _____

13. The monthly payment required by the new second mortgage will amount to $222.98 per month. The total amount of interest paid over the full term of the loan will be:

a. $18,648.34.
b. $15,437.09.
c. $13,428.14.
d. $11,217.60.

14. Review the purchase terms and determine the amount of cash the Maybuys must produce at closing over and above the earnest money deposit. Do not include closing expenses or prorations.

a. $6,000
b. $6,900
c. $7,500
d. $8,900

15. The house purchased by the Maybuys contains 1,500 square feet. The lot is valued at $16,000. What is the cost to reproduce the house new if an accrued depreciation of 4% was applied to determine the house's current appraised value of $61,800?

a. $64,375
b. $74,688
c. $81,042
d. $59,328

Use the following information for questions 16, 17 and 18:

An FHA appraiser has appraised a house at $68,000 (includes closing costs), which is well within the loan maximum in that region. The buyer has found a lender willing to finance the purchase of the house with an FHA mortgage at 9½% interest. A discount of 4 points will be required to conclude the arrangement.

16. The FHA minimum down payment for this property is:

a. $3,900.
b. $3,400.
c. $2,900.
d. $2,040.

17. The cost of the mortgage discount points is:

a. $2,500.
b. $2,584.
c. $2,604.
d. $2,720.

18. The real yield to the lender is:

a. 9.5%.
b. 9.9%.
c. 10%.
d. 13.5%.

19. You purchased a building for 75 percent of its market value. You then found a buyer who bought it from you at full market value. Your percent of profit was:

    a. 35¼%.
    b. 33⅓%.
    c. 29½%.
    d. 25%.

20. An entire farm is divided into separate crop plantings as follows: 140 acres in wheat, 7/16 of the farm in cotton, and 1/8 in alfalfa. The total acreage of the farm is:

    a. 640 acres.
    b. 320 acres.
    c. 290 acres.
    d. 280 acres.

Pre-Test Answer Key

1. $\frac{23}{39}$

2a. $12\frac{5}{12}$

2b. $\frac{1}{18}$

2c. $2\frac{2}{3}$

2d. $\frac{2}{3}$

3. $\frac{75}{16}$

4a. .8

4b. 1.25

5a. $33\frac{1}{3}\%$

5b. 60%

6a. $\frac{3}{2}$

6b. $\frac{1}{20}$

7a. .125

7b. 1.22

8. 149.71

9. 17.956

10. 870.42

11. 17.55 or $17\frac{11}{20}$

12. 200

13. .0106

14. 4.9

15. $25,000

16. $1.20
60%
60%

17. 12

18. 12½%

19. $2,700

20. 9%

21. 8%

22. $150

23. 8,800
45

24. $346.10

25. 315 ft. or 105 yds.

26. 10%

27. $140,000

Chapter Answer Key

Note: If you are unable to figure out how the authors arrived at a particular answer, go back to the "explanation" of the key point in the appropriate chapter and then compare your steps and calculations with those in an "Example" problem that follows each explanation.

CHAPTER 1
Practice Problems:
1-1. Four thousand, two hundred ninety-six
1-2. One hundred eighty-four ten thousandths
1-3. Seven hundred fifty-eight thousand, four hundred twenty

Review Problems:
1. Four thousand, three hundred forty-five
2. Five thousandths
3. Six thousand, two hundred fifty-three and seventeen hundredths
4. Two million, four hundred fifty thousand, fifty
5. Two hundred fifty-eight ten thousandths
6. 3,494.56
7. 14,160,221
8. 98,000,031
9. 2,470.010
10. .6
11. 42.069
12. .7
13. 4.25
14. $16.78
15. $5,000
16. Thousands
17. Hundred thousands
18. Tens
19. Millions
20. Tenths
21. Hundredths
22. Ten thousandths
23. Tenths
24. Millionths
25. Hundred thousandths
26. 69
27. 19,500,000
28. $.74
29. $5.25
30. $63,500

CHAPTER 2
Practice Problems:
2-1. 1 1/8
2-2. 4
2-3. 15/7
2-4. 191/9
2-5. 1/3
2-6. 1/12
2-7. 8
2-8. 12
2-9. 28
2-10. 252
2-11. 22/35
2-12. 41/60
2-13. 18/77
2-14. 2 4/11
2-15. 1/8
2-16. 3 27/35
2-17. 6 2/3
2-18. 2 1/7
2-19. 34
2-20. 1/22
2-21. 25 1/2
2-22. 23.227
2-23. 9.96
2-24. 30.192
2-25. .001
2-26. 3.63
2-27. 25
2-28. 2.5
2-29. .375
2-30. 1 23/100
2-31. 3/5
2-32. 11/100
2-33. 2/25
2-34. 21/200
2-35. .24
2-36. .011
2-37. 12 1/2%
2-38. 23%
2-39. .15; 15/100; 3/20
2-40. 1.2%; 12/1,000; 3/250
2-41. 6 1/4%; .0625; 1/16
2-42. 5%; .05; 5/100
2-43. 50%
2-44. 150%
2-45. 66 2/3%
2-46. 33 1/3%

CHAPTER 3
Practice Problems:
3-1. 4 1/2%
3-2. $243,600
3-3. $5,220
3-4. 15.6%
3-5. 9,700
3-6. $137,500
3-7. 3.5%
3-8. $4,400
3-9. 6%
3-10. $4,875
3-11. $3,012.45
3-12. 5%
3-13. $6,056.25
3-14. $89,000
3-15. $5,444.53
3-16. 7 3/4%

CHAPTER 4
Practice Problems:
4-1. 9 3/4%
4-2. $5,916
4-3. 4 months
4-4. $1,335
4-5. $2,585
4-6. $3,120
4-7. $4,100
4-8. $27,650
4-9. $7,350
4-10. $14,875
4-11. $8,970
4-12. $7,115.25
4-13. $66,215
4-14. $1,758
4-15. 10 3/4%
4-16. $2,965
4-17. 9 1/2%
4-18. 6
4-19. $2,520
4-20. $96; $153.60
4-21. $174; $278.40
4-22. $113.70; $182.08
4-23. $185.52; $296.96
4-24. $252.84; $404.80
4-25. $505.20
4-26. $25.80
4-27. $38,157.84
4-28. $101,992.80

CHAPTER 4 (cont.)
Review Problems:
1. $825
2. $4,440
3. 9 months
4. $300,000
5. $400,000
6. 1 year
7. $1,425
8. $3,395
9. $3,917.50
10. 4
11. $6,720
12. $270 Intang.
    $432 Doc.
13. $48.19
14. $104.89
15. $488.62
16. $36,660.84
17. $132,103.60

CHAPTER 5
Practice Problems:
5-1. .016 (16 mills)
5.2. $731.25
5-3. $400.40
5-4. $368.50
5-5. $401.50
5-6. $32.32
5-7. $20.20
5-8. $493.90
5-9. $229.76
5-10. $143.60

Review Problems:
1. EE - NR
   TAV - E
2. 16.6 mills
3. 44 mills
4. $1,326
5a. $453.20
5b. $84.48
5c. $52.80
6a. $393.25
6b. $191.36
6c. $119.45

CHAPTER 5 (cont.)

7a. .001
7b. .010
7c. .100
8a. 16.589
8b. 3.014
8c. 35.54
 9. $2,511.16
10. $1,310.40
11. $729.60
12. 17.9 mills
13. $62,000
14. $1,431

CHAPTER 6
Practice Problems:

6-1.

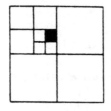

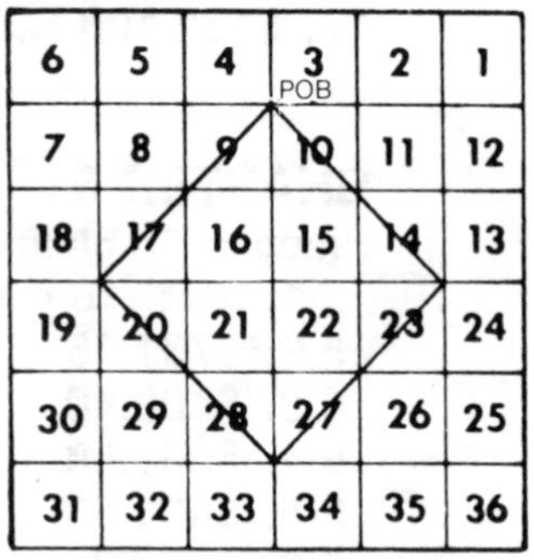

6-2.

6-3. 40
6-4. 40 acres
6-5. 1.02
6-6. 3.2
6-7. SW¼ — 160 acres
6-8. SE¼, NW¼ — 40 acres
6-9. N½, NW¼ — 80 acres
6-10. N½, SW¼, NW¼ — 20 acres
6-11. W½, E½, NE¼ — 40 acres
6-12. W½, W½, NE¼, SE¼ — 10 acres

CHAPTER 6 (cont.)
6-13. SE¼, SW¼, SE¼ — 10 acres
6-14. SE¼, SE¼ — 40 acres
6-15. $64,000
6-16. 80
6-17. $16,000

Review Problems:
 1. 24 miles
 2. 36
 3. 43,560
 4. 640
 5. 40
 6.

 7.

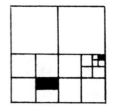

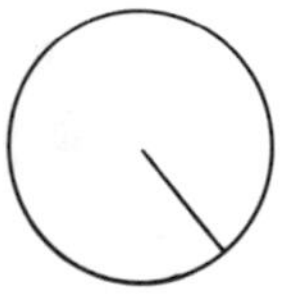

20 acres

 8. 2.5 acres (see figure above)
 9. 60
10. 65
    $975,000
11. 2,750
12. 660 feet
13. $7.20
14. 2
15. 40%
16. 113.10 feet
    1,017.88 sq. ft.
17. 12,566.4 cu. ft.
    94,248
18. $1.35
19. 57,575
20. 1,852 sq. ft.

CHAPTER 7
Practice Problems:
- 7-1. $483,400
- 7-2. 12%
- 7-3. $224,000
- 7-4. $7,668
- 7-5. $1,806,000
- 7-6. $2,816
- 7-7. $67,584
- 7-8. $54,814
- 7-9. $27,427.10
- 7-10. $27,386.90
- 7-11. 38.04%
- 7-12. 2.0
- 7-13. 18.9%
- 7-14. 53.1%
- 7-15. $2,037 loss
- 7-16. $2,850
- 7-17. $77,096
- 7-18. $21,131 increase

Review Problems:
1. 3.33%
2. 25 years
3. 20 years
4. 2.86%
5. 2.22%
6. $57,760
7. $180,000
8. 2%
9. 24%
10. 85%
11. $7,160
12. $11,437.50
13. $112,000
14. 1,935
15. $92,880
16. $101,592
17. $953
18. 132
19. $62,040
20. $153,571.42
21. $153,640
22. 85%

CHAPTER 8
Practice Problems:
- 8-1. $104.85
- 8-2. 65
- 8-3. 221
- 8-4. 167
- 8-5. Debit Buyer $805.20
  Credit Seller $805.20
- 8-6. Debit Seller $691.20
  Credit Buyer $691.20
- 8-7. Debit Seller $353.55
  Credit Buyer $353.55
- 8-8. Debit Seller $115.32
  Credit Buyer $115.32

Review Problems:
1a. Debit Buyer, Credit Seller $136.16
1b. Debit Seller, Credit Buyer $405
1c. Debit Seller, Credit Buyer $247.74
1d. Debit Seller, Credit Buyer $231.85
1e. Debit Seller $440
1f. Debit Buyer $48
1g. Debit Buyer $30
2a. Debit Buyer, Credit Seller $1,988
2b. Debit Seller, Credit Buyer $1,443.95
2c. Debit Seller, Credit Buyer $1,197
2d. Debit Seller, Credit Buyer $169.65
2e. Debit Seller $605
2f. Debit Buyer $89.60
2g. Debit Buyer $56

Post-Test Answer Key

POST-TEST "A"

1. $99,750
2. 264 feet
3. $1,550
4. $20.82
5. $918.75
6. 9½%
7. $4,224
8. 160 acres
9. 73%
10. 12,000 sq. ft.
11. $22,500
12. $4,650 per acre
13. $3.50 per sq. ft.
14. 28,000 sq. ft.
15. $47,500
16. 110 GRM
17. $2,200.95
    9 7/8%
    $2,113.09
18. $36,859 increase
19. Debit Seller, Credit Buyer $269.33
    Debit Seller, Credit Buyer $501.78
    Debit Buyer, Credit Seller $104
20. Debit Seller $194.32
    Credit Buyer $194.32

POST-TEST "B"

1. b
2. c
3. a
4. c
5. c
6. c
7. 23 acres
   $3,450
8. b
9. $15,500
   $3,100
   $6,200
10. Debit Seller, Credit Buyer $1,173.13
11. Debit Buyer, Credit Seller $486.47
12. Debit Seller, Credit Buyer $333.79
13. d
14. b
15. a
16. c
17. c
18. c
19. b
20. b

INDEX

REACTION QUESTIONNAIRE

1. I bought REAL ESTATE MATH at _____
   (name of store/school)

   _____
   (state)   (zip)

2. I used this book in connection with my _____.
   (name of course)

   at _____.
   (name of school)

   __ It was required.   __ It was optional.   __ I found it on my own.

3. The *most* helpful parts of the book:

   _____

   _____

   _____

4. The *least* helpful parts of the book:

   _____

   _____

   _____

5. I would like to see you *change/add* the following:

   _____

   _____

   _____

6. And, I would like to say that:

   _____

_____

date   —*Thank you* for completing and mailing this questionnaire.

fold, tack, and mail

pla
sta
her

TO: Dr. David S. Coleman
Real Estate Education Company
a division of Dearborn Financial Publishing Inc.
Suite 1256
378 Whooping Loop
Altamonte Springs, FL 32701

fold here

from: _____
(optional)

_____

_____

Get the Performance Advantage on the job. . .*in the classroom*

Order Number		Real Estate Principles and Exam Preparation	Qty.	Price	Total Amount
1.	1510-01	Modern Real Estate Practice, 13th edition		$36.95	
2.	1510-02	Study Guide for Modern Real Estate Practice, 13th edition		$13.95	
3.	1961-01	Language of Real Estate, 4th edition		$28.95	
4.	1610-07	Real Estate Math, 4th edition		$15.95	
5.	1512-10	Mastering Real Estate Mathematics, 5th edition		$25.95	
6.	1970-04	Questions & Answers To Help You Pass the Real Estate Exam, 4th edition		$21.95	
7.	1970-06	Real Estate Exam Guide: ASI, 3rd edition		$21.95	
8.	1970-09	Guide to Passing the PSI Real Estate Exam		$21.95	
9.	1970-08	New York Real Estate Exam Guide		$21.95	

Advanced Study/Specialty Areas

			Qty.	Price	Total Amount
10.	1520-02	ADA Handbook: Employment and Construction Issues Affecting Your Business		$29.95	
11.	1560-08	Agency Relationships in Real Estate, 2nd edition		$25.95	
12.	1978-03	Buyer Agency: Your Competitive Edge Real Estate, 2nd edition		$24.95	
13.	1557-10	Essentials of Real Estate Finance, 7th edition		$38.95	
14.	1559-01	Essentials of Real Estate Investment, 4th edition		$38.95	
15.	1556-10	Fundamentals of Real Estate Appraisal, 6th edition		$38.95	
16.	1556-14	How to Use the Uniform Residential Appraisal Report, 2nd edition		$24.95	
17.	1556-15	Introduction to Income Property Appraisal		$34.95	
18.	1556-11	Language of Real Estate Appraisal		$21.95	
19.	1557-15	Modern Residential Financing Methods, 2nd edition		$19.95	
20.	1556-12	Questions & Answers to Help You Pass the Real Estate Appraisal Exams		$26.95	
21.	1551-10	Property Management, 4th edition		$35.95	
22.	1560-01	Real Estate Law, 3rd edition		$38.95	
23.	1556-18	Uniform Standards of Professional Appraisal Practice, 2nd edition		$19.95	

Sales & Marketing/Professional Development

			Qty.	Price	Total Amount
24.	1913-04	Close for Success		$18.95	
25.	1907-06	How to Develop a Six-Figure Income in Real Estate		$22.95	
26.	1909-06	New Home Selling Strategies: A Handbook for Success		$24.95	
27.	4105-09	How to Profit in Commercial Real Estate Investing		$34.95	
28.	1913-01	List for Success		$18.95	
29.	1913-11	Phone Power		$19.95	
30.	1907-05	Power Real Estate Advertising		$24.95	
31.	1926-03	Power Real Estate Letters		$29.95	
32.	1907-01	Power Real Estate Listing, 2nd edition		$18.95	
33.	1907-04	Power Real Estate Negotiation		$19.95	
34.	1907-02	Power Real Estate Selling, 2nd edition		$18.95	
35.	1965-01	Real Estate Brokerage: A Success Guide, 3rd edition		$35.95	
36.	5608-71	Real Estate Investor's Tax Guide		$24.95	
37.	1913-13	The Real Estate Sales Survival Kit.		$24.95	
38.	1978-02	Recruiting Revolution in Real Estate		$34.95	
39.	1903-31	Sold! The Professional's Guide to Real Estate Auctions		$32.95	
40.	2703-11	Time Out: Time Management Strategies for the Real Estate Professional		$19.95	

NEW! Audio Tapes

			Qty.	Price	Total Amount
41.	1926-06	Power Real Estate Listings		$19.95	
42.	1926-05	Power Real Estate Selling		$19.95	
43.	1926-04	Staying on Top in Real Estate		$14.95	

Shipping/Handling Charges	Order shipped to the following states must include applicable sales tax:
$0-24.99 .... $4	
$25-49.99 .... $5	
$50-99.99 .... $6	CA, FL, IL & NY
$100-249.99 .... $8	

Book total _____
Tax _____
Shipping and Handling _____
Less $1.00 off if you fax order _____
Total amount _____

Prices are subject to change without notice.

R93004

Real Estate
Education Company

Where Experts Begin

a division of Dearborn Financial Publishing, Inc.

520 North Dearborn Street, Chicago, IL 60610-4354